YO-ABH-638

PASSAGES OF RETIREMENT

Recent Titles in
Contributions to the Study of Aging

PASSAGES OF RETIREMENT

PERSONAL HISTORIES OF STRUGGLE AND SUCCESS

Richard S. Prentis

CONTRIBUTIONS TO THE STUDY OF AGING, NUMBER 23
Erdman B. Palmore, *Series Adviser*

GREENWOOD PRESS
New York • Westport, Connecticut • London

Library of Congress Cataloging-in-Publication Data

Prentis, Richard S.
    Passages of retirement : personal histories of struggle and
success : Richard S. Prentis.
       p.   cm.—(Contributions to the study of aging, ISSN
0732-085X ; no. 23)
    Includes bibliographical references and index.
    ISBN 0-313-28493-8 (alk. paper)
    1. Retirement—United States—Case studies. 2. Marriage—United
States—Case studies. 3. Retirees—Employment—United States—Case
studies. 4. Age and employment—United States—Case studies.
5. Part-time employment—United States—Case studies. I. Title.
II. Series.
HQ1064.U5P684   1992
306.3'8—dc20   92-1131

British Library Cataloguing in Publication Data is available.

Library of Congress Catalog Card Number: 92-1131
ISBN: 0-313-28493-8
ISSN: 0732-085X

First published in 1992

Greenwood Press, 88 Post Road West, Westport, Connecticut 06881
An imprint of Greenwood Publishing Group, Inc.

Printed in the United States of America

The paper used in this book complies with the
Permanent Paper Standard issued by the National
Information Standards Organization (Z39.48-1984).

10 9 8 7 6 5 4 3 2 1

Dedicated to
the gal from Elyria, Ohio,
my wife, Harriet

Contents

Contents

Preface

Many of us have a desire for some inexplicable reason to write a book. I suppose basically we feel we have a story to tell. Our story arises from where we are coming: professional writers for the money—philosophers to explain belief systems—historians to delineate the past—psychologists to discuss behavior—economists to translate the movement of money—movie stars, celebrities, and now politicians to tell their story known as "kiss and tell."

My reason was to present the life event of retirement as a basis for guidance to those men and women thinking about their future years.

My belief was threefold that future retirees would benefit from my innovative approach to the subject of retirement. First, the fact that I had retired provided hands-on contact with the problems and promises of retirement. Second, my research in the field indicated a need to relate the retirement experience, not from a cohort or statistical standpoint, but rather from the richness of an individual's recollection. Finally, I believe the shared trials, tribulations and triumphs of other retirees suggest approaches to the transition from work to retirement.

Since, to my knowledge, there is no book on the market that addresses retirement in an individual, personal manner, I have gone to the source, actual retirees, to learn of their experiences expressed in their own words.

These conversations provide an opportunity for the reader to share the sentiments of others as they considered leaving their jobs, making the decision to retire, and details of their lives in retirement. Each interview is followed by a short analysis of a salient point arising from the retiree's conversation. The pattern of passages of these retirement experiences include such topics as the decision, work versus retirement, marriage, retirement planning, and leisure.

My procedure was to make contact, by phone or letter, with people who had retired. We met in their homes or some quiet setting. I set up my tape recorder and we talked of the facts, feelings and attitudes they recalled of their journey of retirement.

What these interviewees revealed were often deeply personal memories. I felt they welcomed the opportunity, perhaps for the first time, to express their thoughts on this turning point in their lives. Much to my surprise, particularly after a former president's affair with tapes, no one rejected the idea of having his or her conversation taped. Perhaps there were two reasons for this acceptance of my method of recording their words. First, I was not confrontational, nor did I attempt to probe too deeply into their lives. Second, and perhaps this is basic to human interaction, I encountered a sincere desire on the part of these men and women to be frank, honest, even in disturbing and unsettled situations, in the sharing of this part of their lives.

I explained to everyone the purpose of my work: to assist others in understanding the event of retirement. It is my belief the retirees in this book willingly told their stories in an effort to help others.

Acknowledgments

I have been lucky. If one is fortunate in a lifetime to have one mentor, that is, indeed, a blessing. My good fortune has provided a few people who assisted, encouraged and offered direction to achieve the goal at hand.

Woodrow H. Hunter, of the University of Michigan, a pioneer in retirement education, reviewed some of the early chapters. His enthusiasm and recognition of this method of presenting the retirement experience of others was instrumental in my decision to undertake this book.

Max Brill and Lawrence Lilliston, of Oakland University, were helpful in their way to assist me through graduate school. Max encouraged me to believe I could master beginning statistics, a required rung in the academic ladder, and Larry was my leader as I prepared my master's thesis.

Marilyn Popyk, a published author in the field of computers, led me by the hand through the maze of contacting publishers with the wonderful result of having *Passages of Retirement* published.

Others who were helpful along the way include: David Weiner, formerly of Wayne State University, who mastered the world of computers sufficiently to assist me in various research projects, and Katherine Neil, who transcribed the many taped interviews.

How does one thank the men and women who made this book possible? They talked to this stranger about their lives, openly, freely, sharing their individual experience of retirement. It is my belief that they realize their contributions will provide some guidelines to others on the road to retirement.

I

THE DECISION

"I never gave a single thought to retirement . . . "
"I thought retirement was something to avoid . . . "
"I have looked forward to retirement . . . "
"I thought early retirement was a great idea."
"I had no choice . . . "
"I felt I should take early retirement . . . "
"I thought about retirement 10 to 20 years before . . . "

1

On the Road to Retirement . . .

It was a brisk sunny morning, November 2, 1981. A few oak trees carried their brown leaves; dormant rosebuds awaited another season. The light blue sky was graced by passing misty clouds; the freshness of cool air announced the arrival of fall.

The news of this date in the *New York Times* was not earthshaking: INTERNATIONAL: Soviet Sub Spends Sixth Day Grounded On Swedish Coast . . . Solidarity Chapters in Poland to Continue Strikes . . . Australia, Under New Policy Seeking Americans . . . Asia Urged to End Population Surge . . . NATIONAL: Delay in Taxes Raised Till '83–'84 Backed by Reagan and Dole . . . Profits Off for Many Corporations . . . Treasury Plans Heavy Borrowing . . . REGIONAL: Pennsylvania Inmates Give Columnist List of Demands . . . Improving the Self-Image of Older Women . . . Family Therapy Is Coming of Age . . . Jets Stagger Giants 26–7 . . . Cowboys Triumph Over Eagles 17–14 . . . Thomas Starts with a Bang for Pistons . . . Going North for Grouse . . . LOCAL: Mayor Koch Favored to Win a Second Term.

Just an ordinary day—but this was the day I retired. Now all my part- and full-time jobs were to be memories—a stockboy in a national shoe chain on Saturdays . . . four months in the Allison Tank Plant . . . a three-and-a-half-year stint in the U.S. Army, World War II . . . six months in an advertising agency . . . a year as a Johnson & Johnson sales- man . . . about a year and a half in a scrap yard . . . some thirty years in an automobile dealership.

Now at 61, I was to experience daily living without the stress, the routine, the frustration of work; and without the challenge, the accomplishment, the structure and the meaning of earning a living. Would I be prepared for this turning point in my life? Could I cope? Would I be able to adjust to a day-to-day life where work was no longer the motivating force? If there were no great financial strains would I find pleasure, satisfaction and meaning in my retired years? Would they be the "golden years" as some have suggested, or would I have problems?

The circumstances involving my interest in retirement matters, both personal and social, were the result of returning to college for the second time eight years before I retired. My previous college activity took place some thirty-one years ago in 1942 at the University of Missouri.

At the time I owned a forty-acre "farm" where this city boy had the thrill of watching sweet corn grow six feet high and growing so many zucchini that my friends refused to accept them late in the season. My feeling for the outdoors, the joy of walks in the forest, the sweet taste of hand-pumped water and the passage of seasons were all a meaningful dimension of my life.

My wife, however, thought that if I visited this country place on a full-time basis the joy and pleasure would not be realized or sustained in view of my busy business life. I will never know whether her assumptions were correct, but I followed her general advice and registered at Oakland University, in Rochester, Michigan, for graduate work in developmental psychology. This step was to result in a meaningful avocational interest when I retired.

Since psychology was such a broad field involving human behavior from the beginnings to the end of life, I hoped to focus on some segment where I could learn and possibly make a contribution. Perhaps because retirement education was age-related to the season of life I was approaching, I became interested in researching this area.

Fifty-odd years ago no one was concerned about retirement. People worked as long as they were physically able to; only a privileged few lived without the need to work. Those were the days before pensions, Medicare and Social Security.

Today questions and appropriate answers about retirement are important to everyone. Greater numbers of working men and women are reaching the years of retirement.

It is claimed that by the year 2000, 13.1% of our population, or 34.9 million persons, will be 65 years or older (AARP, "A Profile of Older Americans"). Of equal significance related to our longevity is the fact that an increasing segment of the working population is electing the option of early retirement at 62 or before.

When you consider that our life expectancy, after reaching age 65, is projected as an additional 16.9 years (18.6 years for females, 14.8 years for males), this represents 20 percent of our total life. It therefore seems reasonable and worthwhile to learn something about this period of life that is unencumbered by the role of work.

When I started my work in this field involving workers considering retirement and actual retirees, I came to the conclusion they were viewed as yesterday's children. Limited research had been undertaken to provide insight in to this period of life. Although the term developmental applies to all stages of life, from childhood to the truly elderly, sparse effort has been devoted to studying and understanding the later life cycles. This point was referred to by others: "The study of 'normal' development has seldom gone beyond early adult years, and the great emphasis has been on childhood. The healthy aged tend to be invisible in the psychology of human development, and this is in accord with the general public avoidance of the issues of human aging" (Butler & Lewis, 1973).

It was therefore no wonder that myths about work and retirement had been accepted. It was assumed that work was the central life interest. While work for some people is the most meaningful activity to the period of retirement, either because of the actual work, or the money and the related association of people on the job, certainly it is not the whole story.

The Institute for Social Research (1974) at the University of Michigan reported contrary findings to the overwhelming influence of the work environment. They stated that while "there is interplay between the satisfactions people derive from the different aspects of their lives—work, family, marriage, housing—people reserve their greatest satisfaction from those parts of their lives that are the most intimate and personal."

Stereotypes about the working female population were common. As one researcher noted, there is "an implicit assumption that the working roles of women are relatively unimportant" (Kline, 1975). Working women were supposed to work for different reasons than men, and having dissimilar work patterns, retirement was not seen as an important consideration.

The fact is that women work for the same considerations as men do: to support themselves, often as principal family providers. Many women work full time on a continuous basis regardless of their marital status. Retirement, likewise, is a turning point in their lives.

So much for the unsupported idea of the past about work and retirement. My investigation began fourteen years ago with my assignment as an associate of the Institute of Labor and Industrial Relations, at Wayne State University, Detroit, Michigan, in 1975. I initiated my research with people who were still working. I wanted to understand their thoughts and attitudes toward the future years—their eventual retirement.

Comments from these future retirees ranged from anticipated pleasure to pain. "I view retirement as a natural break in my work career, an opportunity to start a new career in other areas" . . . "retirement is old age, hence I dread it" . . . "another phase of life that can be enjoyable as any, provided one makes the effort to enjoy it" . . . "retirement is a status forced upon persons solely on the basis of age, not physical or mental capacity" . . . "an opportunity to delve into new activities, acquire new skills" . . . "a time of boredom and uselessness."

Here was a beginning picture. This told me in a general way something about the thoughts and attitudes of working people toward retirement. But what were these based on? What was the foundation for anxiety or anticipation about the future?

POSITIVE VIEWS

Retirement for many is thought of primarily as a period of freedom of time and movement. It appears to be an opportunity to do all the things one enjoys. As one person expressed his idea of freedom in retirement: "Sleep till noon and then do any damn thing I please."

Travel is looked on by many as a large part of their retirement activity: "freedom to travel" . . . "travel at a leisurely pace."

Retirement for some working people simply means less pressure, the absence of schedules and less responsibility. They visualize a time of relief compared to their work-life structure and "a chance to slow down."

Some people think of retirement as a time to follow other interests, explore new fields. These activities include: "becoming useful at something not dependent on income" and "doing some socially worthwhile projects."

Retirement is also viewed as an opportunity to spend more time with family and friends.

Some future retirees see retirement as a time to develop and pursue hobbies: "a time to select new ones and to devote full time in this area." To a limited extent mention is made about the future regarding part-time work, study areas, second career activity and volunteering in community and organizational groups.

NEGATIVE VIEWS

Financial concerns are the major consideration about the future. These financial issues relate to people living on a fixed income with no hedge against inflation, the possible discontinuance of Social Security and pensions not rising to accommodate for the increase in prices. Some people worry about the fact they would not be able to maintain a lifestyle they are accustomed to.

The issue of health was a concern about the future in terms of health costs and the absence of anyone to assist and provide care if they became physically or mentally disabled. One man's anxiety was expressed by "physical deterioration due to too much free time."

The perceived burden of time was seen as a problem area in retirement. Some issues mentioned included: "all the time and not enough to do" . . . "intelligent time use so as not to stagnate."

Others wondered about what their activities were going to be in retirement. Such matters as difficulty in keeping busy, staying fully occupied and engaging with people and worthwhile activities revealed uncertainty about future satisfaction: "possibly that my activities will not be as much fun or interesting when they are all I have to do."

The lack of schedules and routines were viewed by some men and women as possible problem areas. Their remarks included: "learning to slow down," "am programmed to a rigid schedule" . . . "coping with a feeling of being unstructured" . . . "adjusting to a non-work schedule."

The question of missing their work was mentioned as they considered the redirection of their lives in retirement. Some comments included: "missing the excitement of work" . . . "accept the fact that my chosen career would come to an end" . . . "I would miss the professional contact and the stimulation of professional activities."

The idea of losing friends and business peers when one retires was seen as a negative aspect in the future: "losing touch with people" . . . "not seeing and meeting people every day" . . . "would miss the daily business contacts."

Attitudes toward aging were revealed when these working men and women thought of retirement. They stated that "our society is geared for younger people; older people are forgotten." Their personal concerns involved such matters as "being considered old" . . . "looking after myself when I can no longer drive a car" . . . "possibility of retiring alone if my wife predeceases me."

Husband and wife relationships were referred to as part of the future retirement scene: "getting along with my spouse when you spend lots of

time together" . . . "learning to live with your spouse all day, every day"
. . . "encouraging my husband to stay active" . . . "possibly that my
spouse may retire at a much earlier age than I can afford to."

Personal feelings about the future were discussed involving challenges,
contributions, and usefulness. Some people felt they would no longer be
contributing to society and that their talents and abilities would not be
needed. Others talked about: "loss of purpose" . . . "adjustment to
self-image and worth" . . . "to maintain a feeling of productivity."

RETIREMENT STUDIES

While at the Institute I developed two areas of inquiry. The first effort
was to ascertain to what degree employers were interested in assisting
their employees plan for the future. This subject was addressed in
"National Survey of Fortune 500 Pre-Retirement Plans and Policies"
(Prentis, 1975). Another area, largely neglected and unexplored, related
to the plans for retirement of working women; these findings were
presented in "White-Collar Working Women's Perception of Retirement"
(Prentis, 1980). These published research projects and others, along with
various retirement seminars at Drake University and the Institute of
Gerontology—the University of Michigan, combined to provide a background and increased understanding of the subject of retirement.

Now that some information had been obtained from working men and
women about their ideas of retirement, I turned to the source—retirees.

If you are in the group that looks forward to retirement, or "never
plan on retiring," or has "never thought about retirement," the lives of
the retirees who made this book possible will assist you in thinking
through your own particular set of circumstances. Some will be rein-
forced in their thinking that retirement is just what they thought it would
be; others will be convinced that they had better work as long as possible.
Whatever your viewpoint on retirement, this will be a learning opportunity about a time of your life quite different from your earlier years.

I wish to make clear this is not a "how-to" book in the conventional
sense, but rather, a book presenting challenges. The first challenge is to
come to your own conclusions about the trials and triumphs of others
with the retirement experience. Although salient points are discussed
following each interview, your own thinking and judgment will contribute
to your learning experience.

The second challenge is personal on your part. Simply stated, this calls
for a life review of the meaning of your work, your attitude toward

retirement, and general plans and preparation for the future. Although our lives and behavior are truly individual, we may benefit, nevertheless, from witnessing the means of others to find purpose and pleasure in their lives.

The final challenge involves your satisfaction or lack of it as you leave the work force and face the retirement years. Whether you have planned specifically or accept retirement as a normal turn of events, awareness of change is all-important. These changes for most people involve financial matters, health subjects, meaningful activities, relationships and your personal self-evaluation in the newfound role of retiree. If you are uncertain about the path ahead for any reason, these challenges present an opportunity to get your personal house in order to take advantage of the opportunities retirement offers.

All methods of research—questionnaires, polls, brief anecdotal reports, statistical summaries and interviews—have limitations. I chose the interview approach, recognizing the boundaries of personal revelation and recollection. My method was similar to what social scientists call "participant observation": "The point of these conversations was to allow people to speak freely about themselves and the circumstances of their lives" (Cottle, 1978). At its very least the words of the retirees are unique as they express the impact of their retirement.

The conversations that follow are a record of events, observations, personal activities, reflections and feelings that relate to the life experience of retirees.

This book consists of interviews with retirees who held a variety of jobs. The people I spoke with included: blue- and white-collar workers—hourly, salaried, and self-employed. At the times of the interviews they had been retired from 2 weeks to 17 years. Their ages ranged from 50 to 82. All names of the retirees, their employers and geographic information has been withheld for reasons of confidentiality. The people I interviewed, in many instances, shared parts of their personal lives and I have respected their privacy.

The retirees were wonderfully cooperative. Many were surprised by what they said. This appeared to be the first time they had reviewed their lives with anyone. From their experiences of both confusion and confidence we may begin to understand this developmental stage of life.

No attempt is made to present a scientific study. The central focus is to relate the process of retirement of people with different ranges of education, income and job type. Most social studies attempt to secure a commonality in the population to be studied, i.e., sex, age, marital status, job type, income, health factors, geographic location. The only requirement for this book was that the person was vocationally retired or had gone back to work after a period of time.

These interviews illustrate the manifold patterns of retirement. Further, I think these retirement profiles offer a glimpse into the lives of people with whom you can relate and identify. They have shared your feelings and questions about the future. They have had your hopes and dreams, as well as your concerns, about retirement. As you might expect, some have adjusted well, while others are frustrated by their mistakes and inability to understand or solve their problems.

What I attempted to talk about with these retirees were their feelings and attitudes as well as the actual events prior to retirement—the decision-making process—and the aftermath of the decision to retire. It is from this total perspective that we have the opportunity to share the experience of others.

We see a relationship between attitudes toward work and retirement. We learn how some retirees felt about early retirement, either elective or mandatory, the extent of their preretirement planning, the attention or lack of it to financial considerations and the influence of health factors.

The retirees relate what prompted them to think about retirement, their major concerns, and who, if anyone, was involved in the decision. Finally, after they retired, we discover what happened—what they do with their time, something of their adjustments. In some instances recommendations are made to others on the road to retirement.

THE FACT OF RETIREMENT

We will all face retirement in our own way, in our own time. Our retirements will be as individual as were our own prior life experiences. While our needs and behavior are products of our environment, an awareness of the similarity of concerns and desires of others are worthwhile to assist us in understanding retirement.

We will all be touched by the event of retirement, either our own or that of important people in our lives, friends and relatives. When we view the retirement of others we are, at the same time, considering the welfare of ourselves. It is clear we do not retire in a vacuum or alone. The step from a formal work activity does not bring an end to our living or remove us from society. Retirement, for most people, is an inevitable life event producing challenges that necessitate adaptation and adjustment that result in pleasant and unpleasant consequences.

These changes, one way or other, affected the lives of these retirees regardless of their type of work or income. Whether retirement was desired or viewed as something to avoid, many factors influenced their satisfaction or lack of it when the work role was over. A retiree's health, a search for some meaningful activity, the degree of spousal interaction and feelings of self-worth all contributed, to some degree, to their adjustment. Those who appeared most successful had achieved a balance between their individual activities and participation in a social setting.

One difficulty in understanding retirement, as well as in being prepared for the actual event, is our lack of exposure to real models—retirees.

Since much of our behavior is learned from our parents and from peers in our own age group, we have the opportunity to observe and learn. These people's patterns are invaluable in our understanding of the stage of life we are in. Our identity, our sense of worth, are established by our own development as well as from the models around us.

Contrary to earlier periods in our lives, when there were those to guide us, retirement is a different matter—an individual task. Many people do not know any retirees. Those who do have some acquaintanceship with it usually do not possess firsthand knowledge of the events and transition to retirement. The interviews that follow will provide some models to illustrate patterns of struggle and success.

As life itself is a journey, let us travel down the road of retirement of others, learning, listening, sharing the path we may someday follow. If a picture is worth a thousand words, what might be the worth of the human voice?

The Retirement Decision

In the best of all possible worlds . . . we would work a given number of years . . . then make our independent decision to retire. But in the real world, not only is our work often a fortuitous affair, but there is no guarantee of our personal prerogative of a retirement decision. We are influenced by the mandates of our employer, fatigue, changes in the work environment, and very important, the state of our health. These factors contribute in some measure to our voluntary or forced decision to retire.

The basis for a decision to retire and its significance is referred to by researchers in the field: "To understand the impact of retirement and how people adjust to it, we need to know why people stop working. What retirement means for the individual is affected by the circumstances surrounding the retirement. His past experience foreshadows the readjustments the retiree must face and in part determines the way he deals with retirement problems" (Streib & Schneider, 1971).

Retirement decisions are made for a variety of reasons. Financial issues lead the list for most people—they have decided they can afford to retire. Whether or not their financial approach is based on sound footing, or whether they have resolved the future use of their time, retirement appears more pleasurable than continuing to work.

Clearly, if a person disliked his or her job, the work environment had changed or become too difficult, these would be sufficient reasons for retirement.

Such matters as job stress, pressure, routine and physical illness are self-evident reasons for leaving one's job. The retirement of one's spouse is often the motive for the working spouse to retire.

Finally, if a person had a desire to make a career change, work part time, or serve in the community, the rationale for retirement from one's major source of employment would be clear.

What is important is that you understand the reason for your decision to retire. This knowledge will contribute to your adjustment and satisfaction with this period of your life.

Ideally, you make the retirement decision independently. When this option is voluntary, your sense of self-worth is secure. The timing of departure and your reasons for leaving the work force are self-determined. Whether you find the same fulfillment that your work provided, or struggle to maintain meaningful involvement in the retirement years, remains to be seen, but at least your independence in decision-making remains secure.

When your future is determined by your employer, resulting in early or mandatory retirement, and is influenced by subtle offers of additional monies, pension improvements or a direct dismissal, the issues you confront are many. You perhaps wonder . . . are you washed up in a work sense . . . were your efforts appreciated during the many years of service . . . is there a meaningful use of your time without your job? You face a personal challenge. You now, in the face of surprise and confusion, must assess your life.

The seven interviews that follow portray individual attitudes and responses to the retirement decision. We witness shock, anger and disbelief, fear of the future, ambivalence in accepting an employer's offer, joyful pleasure, acceptance and role reversal, some realization of physical relief, and the retirement decision focused on prior planning. The retirement categories referred to at the begining of each interview are defined as follows:

Regular: at the age of 65 or later
Early: prior to the age of 65
Voluntary: retirement decision made independently
Mandatory: retirement decision made by employer

The Trauma of Early Mandatory Retirement

Female, 59, single

Education:	high school graduate
Job Status:	specialized hospital administrator for 40 years
Retirement Income:	$25,000
Health:	reported good
Retirement Category:	early-mandatory, retired for 1 year

I hate to say it, but work was my main interest. I loved my job so much that this was the only place I've worked. I was totally dedicated to my work, which I think now was a mistake.

My plan was to avoid retirement as long as possible. Today you are not forced to retire at 65, so I probably would have stayed forever depending on the state of my health.

When I started working here I was paid $150.00 a month. Over the years I worked my way up, so that in the last couple of years I was making $40,000 a year. In the back of my mind I felt I had plenty of time to save for retirement, so I enjoyed spending my money on my family. I really didn't save and that is one of the things that bothers me now.

I certainly did not have any views on early retirement. I did not anticipate retiring until forced to, probably at age 70 or sooner if my health failed.

My activities, other than my work, were involved with my family. We are a close family group and shared vacations and other activities together.

My job was all-important. I did not miss a day's work in 40 years, nor have I ever been late. If anything, they owe me a fortune if they had to pay me for all the hours and days I have come to work.

While I was working I never gave a single thought to retirement. I suppose if I had thought about it I might have ended up in the West with my retired sister. As far as my finances are concerned, I bought some bonds and part of my salary was put in a tax-sheltered annuity by my employer. I know it is a good idea to have a will, but I still haven't gotten around to taking care of that matter. Since I've been retired I have done a lot of traveling and visiting; prior to that time I had not been on a real vacation in years because I was married to my job.

My life, other than my work, revolved around taking care of my parents. My father became a double amputee because of diabetes, so my lunch hour every day for nine years was devoted to giving him his insulin shot and taking his tray to him. My brothers and sisters were married, had their own homes and could not help. I had one unmarried sister, who chose to quit her job to help our parents, so between the two of us we did our best to make life bearable for them. After my father died, my mother became senile and we spent the next nine years taking care of her. That is what I did with eighteen years of my life.

I was hit with mandatory retirement out of the blue. I had finally gotten to the point where I thought I was making big money, then the job was gone and it left me feeling strapped.

I had a feeling that I might be the one to be chopped. I did not have a college degree and I had picked up some skill with the computer systems by on-the-job training. I wondered, could it be me, but then I thought, not me after 41 years and the fine association I had with the doctors.

The only dismissals that I knew about were the administrator of the hospital and the head of the maintenance department, who had 30 years of seniority.

Meetings were scheduled with all assistant managers and coordinators with my supervisor. I was assigned for a one o'clock meeting. My supervisor called me into his office and said, "I really don't know how to go about this." I said to him, "Why don't you just do it the easy way—do I have a job or don't I?" He replied, "Unfortunately, no."

I didn't want to cry, because I'm not the crying type, but I felt a cold sweat. He looked so distressed I thought he was going to cry. I asked, "What do we do now?" He replied, "Well, there are certain things, but don't you want to talk about it?" I said, "What is there to talk about—is it going to change anything?"

He said, "Not really." I asked him if there was a chance I could possibly have a job at the front desk doing clerical work. He said, "No, that position has been cancelled." I then inquired whether I could have the job held by a 75-year-old woman. Again he said, "No, because as soon as the computers come in her job will be finished." Finally, I asked, "Is there any place in the hospital for me after 41 years?" He said, "No, they are not hiring now and they are not transferring positions."

I was then escorted to another office where I met a man from the Human Resources Department. I signed various papers. He stated that I was going to get unemployment compensation and separation pay for one year.

I did get paid for that year, which was very nice of them, but I think it was their way of white-washing the whole thing. The truth of the matter is stated in the supervisor's manual that salaried employees are entitled to separation pay based on their years of service; I was entitled to a year's separation.

I was then asked for my name badge, which functions as a key to the enclosed parking area. I asked how I was supposed to get my car. I was told, "That will be taken care of." My supervisor came into the office at the end of this conversation and stated, "We would like you to leave the hospital now." I asked if I could go to my office to get my purse and a few personal pictures. His answer was, "You are not supposed to go back to your office. We will walk you out to the door. Anything you need, someone will bring it to you."

They walked me out through one of the back doors. I was not permitted to walk down the main department hall. I knew that outside consultants hired by the hospital told them exactly what to do; they had no choice.

A friend and fellow worker brought my car to the main entrance and drove me home. My head was filled with all sorts of thoughts . . . did they think I was going to steal something from the goddamned hospital after 41 years . . . I couldn't believe what was happening to me . . . I couldn't believe my supervisor would do that to me, but he carried it out to a "T". He was not happy about it, but he did it.

While my friend drove me home, I could not say a word. I thought for the first time, "I'm out of work." It was terrible. I don't know if I was in a state of shock; I didn't become violent but if I had had a gun in my hand I probably would have shot everybody in front of me. I realized that the 41 years I had given to the hospital added up to one sentence, "We're going to walk you out the door," like a prisoner.

For the first few days I couldn't even think to do anything. I just sat. I would get up at the same time as if I was going to work, then I remembered I don't have to get up. I couldn't sleep, or stay in bed, or stay in the house. I walked around outside. All I could think of was why, why?

A week after I was dismissed, my friend who had driven me home from the hospital came over to talk about the situation. She said my former supervisor asks her every day how I am getting along. Later in the afternoon when I was forced to retire, she said, he broke down and cried, and said that was the hardest thing he ever had to do. I know he had no choice in the matter.

To be very honest, I don't want to be retired from my job. I would like to continue working at what I was doing. I can't see going out and just getting a job somewhere and starting from scratch.

My biggest problem has been adjusting to the fact that I was not employed. It has taken a long time. I still get up in the morning at the same time as before and then I remember, "You are not working." I feel useless; I was depressed for a long time.

Since I retired I have been involved with visiting and providing some care for two of my brothers. Getting a taste of traveling has been wonderful, but this has to be limited because of my finances. I know I will never starve, but I hate to think I would have to leave my home and live with someone because of my financial situation.

I think forced retirement is not really like retiring in the usual sense. I have in the back of my mind that I was made to retire; this feeling never leaves you.

My advice to others about planning for their retirement is. Don't be the same sucker I was. I gave my heart and soul to my job and there was no appreciation. I know I am bitter about what I went through, but the same thing can happen to anyone and a person should be ready for it. Be prepared; don't be a fool. If you've got a husband all this is not so critical. But if you are on your own, you had better think about what could happen.

ARE YOU PREPARED FOR EARLY MANDATORY RETIREMENT?

Every day someone is hired, someone is fired. We know something about the hiring process, the application, the interview, the reference checks, perhaps a second interview. But we know relatively little about how people are fired.

Dismissal procedures vary considerably across the business spectrum. Small companies, where the boss often knows the first names of many of the employees, have their patterns of letting people go. Large employers, because of the size of their work force, employ different methods of dismissal.

This interview graphically illustrates one dismissal method: The employee clearly had no choice, and the immediate effect and aftereffect on the employee.

Employers, generally, may fire anyone as long as their dismissal action is not based on violations of the National Labor Relations Act, the Civil Rights Act, union agreements, and do not intend to replace the dismissed employee who was let go without cause.

Whether this employee of 41 years had unreasonable expectations about her job future, based on service, loyalty and devotion to the work, remains an unanswered question in today's business environment. Likewise, through the emotional upheaval she felt during and following the meeting with her supervisor, she realized he was merely following orders—directions from an outside consultant.

The implication of this early mandatory retirement incident suggests the possibility of your dismissal at any age and without cause. Although you may view this outcome as unlikely, constant vigilance about your finances and the market for your job skills will give you some degree of confidence in knowing you will be able to cope with an unexpected dismissal.

4

The Inevitability of Retirement

Male, age 75, married, two children

Education:	college graduate
Job Status:	dentist, 52 years
Retirement Income:	$30,000
Health:	reported poor
Retirement Category:	regular-mandatory, retired for 6 months

I loved working; that was, next to my wife and family, my first love. My work was my hobby; I had no other hobbies.

When I was in general practice, I didn't have the same interest in my profession as I had when I began working in a specialized field of dentistry. The reason for this change came about eleven years ago when I went in full time at a local hospital and began working on things I had always wanted to do. The reason why I couldn't do this type of work before was because of the need of supporting a family. Because of the hospital arrangements, I was able in my later years to devote full time to this type of work.

I was able to eliminate general practice and devote myself to people with facial deformities. I am considered a maxillofacial prosthodontist. I was the only one in my state doing this type of work. There were very few men throughout the country in this particular specialty. My work was in rebuilding their face and mouth to as near normal as possible.

My inspiration for this type of work came during World War I. I attended lectures by the outstanding plastic surgeon in this country. He inspired me that this was the work I would have liked to do. The compensation for this work is very limited. I also had training in this field in World War II.

I thought retirement was something to avoid as long as possible. In fact, I had never expected to retire. I expected to remain working. I was assured by the hospital that I could stay as long as I wanted. The retirement age at the hospital is 65. I went to work for them when I was 64. I didn't even think about retiring when I became 65, and they didn't say anything to me. They wanted me to stay on because I couldn't be replaced. There was nobody around who could handle this type of work. But a young man came into the field about two years ago, and when I retired at the hospital's suggestion, he took over. I had no feelings, no idea that I was ever going to retire until I had to—I mean either through illness or death. Actually, I was in good health and I felt I could go on this way forever, without anything to stop me, but unfortunately my health changed this picture.

I always felt that anybody who was productive and who had a skill, particularly a skill like mine, should keep on working. I still feel a bit of a guilt as far as leaving some of my patients, although my health doesn't permit me to continue. I feel these people need somebody with the experience to take care of their needs. People who have these deformities need constant attention. They have to be reexamined regularly to see that the cancer doesn't reappear.

I had no other hobbies through the years except my work. When I came back from the service, I set up a little laboratory in the basement in our home. I used to putter and work there Saturdays and Sundays. Later when we moved into a nicer home, I set up a beautiful laboratory; it was very well equipped. I loved to be in my laboratory working on the weekends.

We had friends, and we used to go out and socialize on occasion, but we weren't cardplayers, and we didn't socialize with club activity. My main interest was my work, and my wife has always been very tolerant in this respect. If she hadn't been, I would have been in trouble.

The fact that I had set up the laboratory at home was another thought I had, that in case I was forced to retire, this would be where I would spend my time and use my workshop at home as a hobby. I would continue to keep my finger in the pie. I had always felt as long as I was in good health, retirement was to me a dirty word.

I never did any retirement planning because I never cared to leave my profession and retire to Florida or California, as many of our friends have done. Our legal affairs have been taken care of. Our will has been rewritten and our children and grandchildren provided for.

I never made a lot of money. I was never a high-fee person when I was in practice. My investments were very poor. I can't remember where I have ever made anything on investments. As far as anything that we have in reserve, we have both worked very hard for it. My wife has been teaching for 30 years. We haven't denied ourselves or our children anything, and we have a little set aside for our old age.

We thought that in our retirement, provided we were frugal, we would be able to manage retirement and remain on the same level as we did when I was working.

My retirement was mandatory, because they found a replacement. I would still have been there today, ill health or no ill health, if they hadn't found a replacement. When I became ill, my salary went on just the same, and would have gone on if my health had been sufficiently good where I could return.

When they told me that I was going to be retired, I was sick and depressed. I felt very badly about it and I thought I wouldn't be able to take it, but I guess my health was the one thing that made me realize that there comes a time when you have to accept it.

Our major concerns were whether we would be able to keep up. I hadn't stopped to analyze our financial position, and I didn't want to end up with having to drop our way of living to a lower level. Another thing I thought about was that as I aged, would my mental capacities remain normal. I have always heard the expression that if you retire you deteriorate and die.

There was a little discussion with my wife about my retiring. Of course, my health was so poor at the time that we could see no other way and I simply had to accept it. My wife was disappointed. She wondered what would happen to me, because I had been an active person; now we would be together 24 hours a day, and probably would get on each other's nerves. We will be married 50 years in a few months, and she was afraid that this might end our life together in an unhappy way. She thought it was an injustice. She thought that I should be there forever. I tried to explain that I was very fortunate, that at my age they thought enough of me to keep me on up to this time.

The only thing that I have reduced since my retirement is my level of giving. The charities we have spread out very thin, and now we have reduced it to where it is not going to hurt.

I am depending upon my Social Security and that of my wife, as far as income. I also have a small Army pension, and we have not had to go into our savings. We are hoping that we don't have to. We have had to partially support our daughter and help her for years and years, and so far she is getting more in a position to take care of herself.

Our expenses have always increased each year, but we have been frugal. We are holding our own pretty well. We won't have to dip into our principal unless we buy some luxuries.

Most of our friends have moved away to Florida. We have very few retired friends here.

After retirement became a fact, I stayed awake at nights thinking about it, and wondered what would happen to me physically. Financially I wasn't too worried. I even expected that physically, as soon as I was able, that I would go in and act as a consultant at the hospital. I could always go in and put in two days a week and make my life more interesting.

My only problem since retiring is trying to regain my health. I have worked for so many years. I think if one is physically able, it is a much more enjoyable and rewarding life to continue working and not retire. My father was 97 years old when he passed away; he never retired. He worked when he was 90 years old. He got a job in a factory and worked in order to earn some extra money. I guess it is instilled in the family.

I still feel and hope that I will return to working a few days a week, and that is the only thing I am looking forward to at the present time.

I have no other activities since my retirement than health activities. I am up at five-thirty or six o'clock in the morning and I can't wait until I get my medication, and that keeps me busy practically all day long. I go to the hospital for therapy. At first, when I retired, I would help about the apartment. I have always detested having household help. When I am home and I watch the way they work, it bothers me. I told my wife that I would do the carpet sweeping and some of the dusting, and we have gotten along beautifully. We have household help once in a while when we need to do the heavy work, but now since I have been ill I have to give that up.

I have made a lot of plans to attend various group meetings when I feel better. I am a member of a number of organizations. I still plan to attend everything I can professionally, whether I am working or not.

It has been a rough adjustment, only because of my health. Right now I have become somewhat accustomed to it, and I don't feel as badly as I did at first. I was lost and depressed, and I thought this probably was the end. Now I don't feel that way.

Since I retired, one of the most pleasant aspects is spending more time with my children and grandchildren, and this is enjoyable. I also think I understand my wife better now than I ever did before.

Most of our friends are younger people. I don't know what it is about me, but they must like us because they call on us and we see them frequently.

It is my opinion that if you are happy and well adjusted in your work or your profession, even on a limited basis, I would say remain active. I think that is a good mental therapy as far as life enjoyment and you are doing some good in this world, and that's what you are here for.

If my health gets reestablished in part, I plan to go back on a part-time basis.

MUST THE RETIREMENT DECISION BE FACED BY EVERYONE?

Mandatory retirement occurs for reasons other than age. This fact is often overlooked, particularly by those with high work motivation. The usual idea of mandatory retirement, whether it is early or at age 70, is based on the employer's decision.

In this case history, although this 75-year-old interviewee possessed a needed skill, and notwithstanding his poor health, the hospital's decision was based on the availability of a young, competent replacement. It is not uncommon for individuals whose lives are work centered to have the attitude that they cannot be replaced and that they can go on forever. Such viewpoints are unrealistic.

It must be recognized and accepted, regardless of the employment status of working for others or being self-employed, that changes occur in many ways. The failure to perceive one's indispensability in the work scene, or even the natural process of aging with its concomitant physical decline, makes for a poor retiree prospect. Not only are changes inevitable in the health of an individual, but change takes place in terms of skill needs sought and discarded by the requirements of society.

This man's expression, that "I never would have retired," summing his work-life philosophy, did not alter the hard facts of the case. The hospital had overlooked his age for many years past 65, but had found a replacement. His health for six months prior to the final retirement date had been too poor to allow him to work. The combination of these events resulted in confrontation with retirement.

This man's attitude toward his work, the idea of continual work and rejection of retirement, the influence of his 90-year-old father's lifestyle, and a viewpoint of a link between retirement and death, were sufficient cause for personal loss of order and meaning in his life. It is interesting to note that the only thing he looked forward to, in the final analysis, was some improvement to the point where he could continue his specialty on a part-time basis.

5

Considerations of an Early Retirement Offer

Male, age 59, married, one son

Education: high school graduate, two years vocational school

Job Status: auto service management, 24 years with an automotive manufacturer

Retirement Income: $20,000

Health: reported good

Retirement Category: early-voluntary, decision to retire made two weeks prior to interview

My first reaction to the idea of early retirement, when it was presented to me, I could best describe as though somebody had hit me on the head with a two-by-four. While I had a reason to believe that I would be contacted because of the other activity going on, it was just a question of wait and see, or will they get to me. But even with that thought in the back of my mind, it had quite an impact. I was advised that they wished to discuss it with me, and since retirement income figures were not available at that time, I spent an anxious period waiting to see what our income future would be. There was a rather difficult day or two until we actually knew what the figures were going to be and we could digest and understand them.

After I got the figures I had a week of total confusion. It took me a week to make my ultimate decision. I consider myself extremely fortunate in counseling with my wife, because her reaction was that the final decision had to be mine. She voiced her opinion to the extent that she hoped I would take the retirement offer which would enable me to take things a little easier. There was a lot of moral support in my final decision.

For the week's time, I was back and forth to both extremes. I definitely was not going to take the retirement; I definitely was; and back and forth as often as probably ten-minute intervals. When I finally made the decision in favor of retirement, I still had probably a ten-percent reservation, and at this time, two weeks later, I still have reservations.

I felt rather optimistic about the whole thing because I had the confidence that I would seek other employment on a reduced hour basis. I felt that there might be several opportunities for me to have some further retirement income. I think that without that feeling I perhaps would have gone the other way and not accepted the retirement, or if I had, I'd have been extremely cautious about the future, thinking that this is the end of the line.

I talked with a few friends and purposely did not seek advice, because I had reached the state of utter confusion without any other opinions to further add to my problem. I talked of it in quite lengthy detail with my son. He thought I would be smart to take it. He felt there must be some good opportunities for me, at least in the immediate future, along with the retirement income. Coworkers were vitally interested in my reaction, as to just what was taking place. Some of those people will be faced with a decision of the same nature, not immediately, but down the line. I think there was a personal interest.

One of my major concerns was severing the relationship with a good employer. I think employer relationships make you question whether severing that relationship is the right move, regardless of the financial aspects.

When I made the final decision toward retirement, I continued to feel edgy. For some reason or other, I had the strong feeling that I had to locate with someone else before my actual retirement date. I had a feeling of insecurity if I did not make the connection. I guess that comes from my idea that it is always easier to find a job when you are presently employed than when you are unemployed and looking for a job.

Some of my insecurity is a need and a desire to want to do something, or I guess the desire to feel needed. There is a certain financial aspect to it because of our retirement income. Although we can manage on it, if necessary, I would be quite disappointed just having that as total income, even though it would be sufficient to get by on. I guess I have the feeling that I am not ready to be put out to pasture yet.

I am not one who has great plans or enjoys hobbies. If I were in total retirement at this time I think I would have some difficulty in filling my time with activities totally away from some kind of employment, partial or full time.

My immediate plans are to consummate some further immediate employment, on a part-time basis, where I might have a little more free time to do some of the things we have not been able to do with full employment. I am prepared, if necessary, even to go back to full-time employment, but it would not be my preference. I would like to work for three days, if possible, and have four days free to do a little bit of traveling and enjoy some things with my wife. My wife and I had always hoped when retirement came we would be able to travel. We have longingly looked at motor homes as the ideal way in which we would like to see more of this country. But that sort of thing is beyond our reach, at least at this time, so it probably will not materialize; but maybe some time in the future we can pursue these plans.

While I was working I had not done any serious retirement planning. I had set a tentative target date of 62 for retirement, but still there were no real strong plans made for retirement.

My company did not offer any sort of voluntary preretirement planning program, but if they had, I would have been interested, and I would have participated. I would have to think that it would be very beneficial to anyone coming up to retirement to have some guidance toward their planning. I am sure there are some people who have very definite and specific plans for retirement, but I think that they would be pretty much in the minority. I don't think the average person makes specific plans, and perhaps some guidelines along the line in earlier years would be very beneficial.

I have looked forward to retirement, but this came on me a little more quickly than I was prepared for. However, I am not sure that I would have had very precise plans even if I had continued to work the other three years.

I am quite proud of my association with the company I worked for. I think they have always been fair with me. I think their early retirement offer is very fair and equitable. I have no ill feelings toward the company whatsoever, and I sincerely feel that the offer of early retirement was only an offer. I feel that the final decision was mine and that they would have abided by my decision either way.

WHAT ARE SOME CONSIDERATIONS OF AN EARLY RETIREMENT OFFER?

The idea of early retirement with pay would, at first glance, appear to be a blessing to anyone. Further, this offer by the employer was presented on an elective basis, so that freedom of choice was allowed; the employee could continue to work or retire. The issues involved with this man's decision to elect early retirement elicited his attitude toward the will and the need to work, the question of the readiness to retire, and the adequacy of his preparation for the future.

He was confused for a number of reasons. When the early retirement offer was presented by his employer, specific income figures were not available, thereby causing some degree of anxiety about his financial future. Further, some ambiguity surfaced because of the desire for additional income, the need to be part of a work activity, the possible problem of filling time in retirement, and resistance to the idea of being "put out to pasture."

But the question remains, why, after 24 years of employment with a company he respected, where a satisfactory job status had been attained, did this man choose early retirement?

This early retirement appears primarily to be a business decision. The immediate benefit from a financial standpoint is clear. His election of early retirement resulted in his receiving 65 percent of his normal salary for a period of six years, until age 65. The combination of this supplemental retirement income, in the range of $11,390, along with additional monies from another job, would allow a continuation of his general standard of living, and reduce his former work load.

6

Benefits of Voluntary Retirement

Female, 50, single

Education:	high school graduate
Job Status:	production controller, 30 years with automobile manufacturer
Retirement Income:	$6,000
Health:	reported good
Retirement Category:	early-voluntary, retired for 3 years

My job in production control was interesting, it was a challenge, but it was mainly a man's position. There are more women breaking into it. To be very honest, what with the new age of computerization, I started looking forward to retirement five years ahead of time. My job became nerve-racking after we started using computers, because if the computer goes down or somebody pushes the wrong button and your information is lost, you have a real problem. I thought early retirement was a great idea. If you stop to think about it, there were a lot of people like my dad who passed away exactly eleven months after his retirement party.

I've always had a lot of interests, so I wasn't worried about what I would do with my time when I retired. I used to be a member of various union committees when I was working. Photography has always been a number-one interest and I've always been interested in politics.

Most of my friends were made on the job. If we did anything, it was mostly with people whom we worked with.

My idea of retirement was that it would give me freedom to do what I wanted to do. If you wanted to sleep until noon, fine. If you wanted to take off, make a spur-of-the-moment decision to take off and go somewhere, you could. There would be no one standing over your head saying you have a deadline to meet.

I planned my retirement. Before I retired I bought all the high-priced items: the new TV, the VCR, the new car and camera equipment. Since I live with my mother, the rest of my money is used to pay part of household expenses.

I could hardly wait during the last six months for my 30 years to be up. The company was cutting more and more people. The pressure was great and this helped me make my decision.

Retirement has been a wonderful thing. I can't understand people who say they can't find anything to do. There are millions of things to do. If you don't like arts and crafts as I do, you can always be a volunteer or a worker in a hospital or children's home. If you are one of those who just wants to lay back—fine.

My health is a lot better since I retired. Now there is no stress, my nerves are better; I feel very good. I am busy. First comes the housework, the grocery store, the yard work—the major things come first. Then comes the relaxation, the therapy to be calm, then the hobbies.

The only thing that I miss are the people I used to work with. Their hours and jobs are changed, so it is hard to stay in contact with them. But, as far as the job is concerned—forget it.

I probably would have retired sooner if I could have managed it financially. When I worked it was eight hours a day, sometimes six days a week, and then you've only got Sunday. Life is too short; there are too many things in life you can enjoy other than work. If they could ever come through with a pension of 25 years and out, I think it would be worth it for the people.

The union and the company offered some classes to help us prepare for retirement. They warned us to make sure if we intended to move to another state, like Florida or Arizona, not to sell your home—go there for six months, see if you can take the climate. I took these classes close to the time I retired.

WHAT IS THE RATIONALE FOR AN EARLY VOLUNTARY RETIREMENT DECISION?

The retirement decision and subsequent consequences are often founded on whether the decision is voluntary or mandatory. When the option of early or regular retirement is elected by the employee, freely with no strings attached, there is an optimistic outlook. This personal decision provides for the choice of appropriate timing by the worker. It assures clear reasoning for the election of this option based on the expectation of sought-for lifestyle changes.

The enthusiastic outlook of this "30 year and out" retiree reflects varied influences: the job as being clearly the means to an end, her father's pattern, some effects of the computer age, and a strong desire to live her life without the constraints of work.

As she states her position on early retirement, 30 years and out, she not only thought it was a great idea, but viewed 25 years and out, with a pension, as something "worthwhile for the people." The fact that her father had passed away some eleven months after he retired emphasized the finiteness of life and encouraged her thoughts about retirement.

The emergence of the computer as the contemporary tool of our society is clear. However, to the extent its recognized efficiency is appreciated, the question of stress on the worker in some jobs remains unknown. Obviously, this retiree's work was pressured by "the age of computerization" and fostered the idea of retirement five years ahead of time.

What with her retirement planning achieved of purchasing expensive items while she was still employed, possessing a variety of interests, and realizing physical relief from the job, it would appear she has realized her dreams in retirement.

7

Avoidance of a Retirement Decision

Male, 61 years old, married, four children

Education:	college graduate
Job Status:	drafting supervisor for 16 years
Retirement Income:	$20,000
Health:	reported good
Retirement category:	early-mandatory, retired for 6 months

My work was my main interest, because it was a form of earning a living, and consequently had to be a primary interest. On the whole, I felt successful and satisfied with what I was doing. I started in drafting and worked my way up. I earned a degree while I was working.

Frankly, I was looking forward to retirement when I got to be 65, because I had been in the game for such a long time. I felt that being 61 now, four more years of work would be just fine, and I would be ready to retire at 65.

My job didn't have any bad effect on my health, but there were periods when I was working under high tension; but on a permanent basis the job didn't interfere with my health.

Before I retired, outside of my work, we would socialize with friends, I would play golf, and I fished. I also went to lectures whenever there was the opportunity.

I had hoped to do a lot of traveling when I retired, because I was interested in historical things, and I hoped to see more of the country.

I anticipated that I might have a problem when I retired. I had always heard and read that unless you have some sort of a hobby to keep you busy after you retired, you would deteriorate rapidly. I hadn't prepared for that because outside of golfing and fishing, I don't have any hobbies to keep me busy.

Before I retired, I really hadn't done any serious retirement planning. I had an estimate, or you might say guesstimate, of my total net worth, but I really never sat down and figured out what our general living expenses were, or what it would really cost me after I retired.

Actually, early retirement was presented twice to me by my company. The first time, it came as rather a surprise. I had a choice at that time whether I wanted to retire or not. I wasn't ready for retirement at that time, so I turned it down. The department that I worked in was dependent on outside contracts, even though it was part of this large company. The company took the attitude that as long as we were able to procure contracts, and were able to remain self-sufficient, they were happy to have us go along on this basis. But, due to the world situation and changes in government, the contracts that we had declined in number, and we had to cut back on personnel. We were at one time quite large, and became progressively smaller and smaller. Now the first time I was offered retirement was one of those times when they were cutting back on personnel. They figured they would ask all those people who were 55 and over if they would take early retirement.

I was about 58 or 59 at the time. I was offered an option of early retirement because my department was going to be phased out. They planned to retire just about everybody over 55, including the general manager and the chief engineer and supervisors. They had to take their retirement. I was a little frightened the first time that this retirement offer was made, because I had made no plans for retirement and I didn't know what I could do and what I would have to face in retirement. That's primarily why I turned it down. Also, our girls were going to college, and as a result, because our expenses were high, I felt that I couldn't retire at that particular time.

The second proposition was mandatory. I had no choice. I was concerned again about what I would do with myself. If I retired with the cut in income, I was wondering just how I was going to have to budget myself in the future. At that time, the personnel manager made a passing remark that if I was interested, they would keep me on in another department of the company. I would have to take a reduction in pay and go back on the drawing boards again. I think I was a little too old to do that, so I turned that offer down.

I talked the matter over with my wife, but no one else. She said that if I had to retire, "just to go ahead and retire." She didn't press me to go out and get another job. She was satisfied to have me home.

I didn't think that we would have to live on a reduced standard of living. Since our girls have gotten married and left home, our expenses have been cut considerably. So, although my income was cut, I still thought I could maintain our standard of living. After I became 65, I would imagine my income reduction from my salary will be about sixty percent. I had an idea of what my income would be at that time, because the company gave us annual reports as to what to expect when you get to be 65. I expected our expenses to drop when I retired.

I really hadn't done any retirement planning. I toyed with the idea a little bit, but I figured I still had a few years and I was going to look around for something to do, but this thing hit me all of a sudden.

Frankly, I didn't know how to go about planning for retirement. My company didn't offer any sort of program, but I think it would have been helpful if they had. I think if they had had something to help you figure out your money planning or budgeting for whatever income you had, and help you set up a program of activities that you might engage in, and how you might actually spend your time, it would have been a big help.

I really wanted to avoid retiring as long as possible, because I had always worked. Ever since I was a youngster I had worked, and I didn't know what would happen if I suddenly had to stop working.

When I was officially retired, I sat down with my wife and tried to figure out what I was going to do. In view of the fact that she works, I told her that now, in essence, she is supposed to be the breadwinner; I would reverse roles with her. I would take over the upkeep of the house, I would do the cleaning and the laundry and the cooking and the shopping, and other things that had to be done. This keeps me busy, it keeps me active, and I also have time for other hobbies such as golfing and fishing. I golf in the fine weather. I manage to get out a couple of times a week because I have set up a system to clean the house. Since we don't have any small children, the house doesn't need much maintenance as before. I have found myself quite active in this role.

I had hoped to do some traveling, but since my wife works, we have to stay close to home. What with the reversal of roles, we are really keeping the same routine as we had previously, except I stay home and do the housework, and my wife continues the job she had before I retired.

Since I reversed roles with my wife and I now have the house to look after and the shopping and cooking, I found out that really a woman's work is never done. There is always something to be done here, but I found that I have time for other activities. I have to do the outside gardening work, so I am busy most of the time.

When I first retired, it was a very frustrating experience, because I had been used to working all the time, and through the years had gotten into this routine. Getting up and going to work in the morning, and tackling the problems of the day, and then all of a sudden, this pattern changes. I felt sort of lost, but after a period of time I got used to it and the feeling passed.

My wife tells me she never had it so good since I took over her role in the family.

The first three months were frustrating. Now I have gotten used to it and am beginning to enjoy it. I can now go out and do things that I couldn't do before when I was tied down with a job. On Monday mornings I am now able to go to a lecture and I am able to sign up for various classes.

The most difficult thing about retirement for me is getting used to retirement when you are not prepared for it. It takes a period of time to become adjusted. In my case, I would say it took about three months. When I retired I had the spring and summer months to work in, but I don't know how I am going to be able to face things when winter comes and I am shut in. I have been toying with the idea of maybe going out and getting a part-time job. I don't want a full-time job. This would keep me occupied for a while, during the winter months, and when spring comes, I would drop the job.

When I retired, I did miss the regularity of my work, but I have gotten used to it. In fact, I have had to set up a schedule for myself for this housework.

I am going to take up ceramics, and my wife has gotten into plants and she wants me to make pots for her. She also wants me to get started into macrame. This is a type of knot-tying hobby, and I anticipate this will sort of keep me occupied for a while.

I think that if you had planned early retirement, it would give you the opportunity to do things that you couldn't do while you were working. If you have set up a retirement plan, and have an adequate income and are not tied down with children, this gives you an opportunity to get out and do some traveling and see some things that you couldn't see before while you were working.

I don't think that I would have retired before I was 65 because I think a person should try to remain active as long as he possibly can. On the other hand, sometimes I think that if you can afford it, taking early retirement is a good idea because it gives you an opportunity to enjoy things when you are younger, instead of waiting until you are too old.

I feel I have had a successful life. I have had a very happy life, and I don't think I have ever wanted for anything. I have always made an adequate income so that we could get what we wanted.

I think if I had my choice, I would have continued working because I had set my goal at 65. But because I had to take early retirement, four years before I anticipated, this set my plans back a little bit. I will have to replan. I think if I had done some retirement planning I would have been able to slide smoothly into it without any frustrations or inhibitions. If you could get somebody to plan something for you and have a goal set in mind, when you reach your objective, which is retirement, then you are really happy and are looking forward to it.

ARE YOU PREPARED FOR MANDATORY RETIREMENT?

Early retirement propositions offered by employers often appear in two forms: one as an option, the other as a mandated decision to separate the employee from the job. Few workers are presented with early retirement twice by their employer. The conversation of this retiree provides some insight into forced retirement, where, after refusing the first offer, he was confronted with the company's mandatory decision.

Although this man stated he looked forward to retirement at 65, prior to the first offer of early retirement, he recognized his concerns about the years ahead. He anticipated problems of activity, was uncertain about financial matters, and was somewhat fearful about what the future years would hold. His lifelong pattern of getting up and going to work now presented the confusion of new routines with his early retirement.

The question remains, at what point is it wise to think through the decision to retire? Those issues which appeared troublesome contributed to his apprehension about retirement when he received the initial option. No difference was apparent when he was mandatorily retired three years later. If, as he stated, retirement is the goal, then it certainly behooved him to address all dimensions of retirement prior to electing or accepting early retirement.

8

Option of 30 Years and Out

Male, 65, married, three children

Education:	high school graduate
Job Status:	machinist, gauge repair, 30 years with an automobile manufacturer
Retirement Income:	$12,000
Health:	reported fair
Retirement Category:	early-voluntary, retired for 12 years

When I first started working, the job was a means to an end—I had a family to support. When I got my skilled job, I was interested and enjoyed my work. I put my all into it; I gave them eight hours of work.

My job as a repairman brought me into contact with a lot of people and I made a number of friends. When I retired, my friends from the production department and the skilled trades donated to a retirement gift.

When I was working, I really looked forward to retirement. We had our house paid for and the bills were getting paid, so we made the decision that we could retire and live on our income. Retirement meant that we wouldn't have to get up early in the morning and go to work, although I enjoyed my job. The job was getting more difficult because of the training and schooling involved, and at my age of 53, I couldn't comprehend any more.

I felt I should take early retirement to make room for the younger people. They had no chance of getting better jobs until the older people retired.

I really didn't have many interests. It was mostly maintaining our home, cutting the grass, doing a little fishing and going to the theatre.

Retirement to me meant I could take it a little easier. If I wanted to go somewhere, I could go, or take a trip and stay longer periods without any problems. When we retired, we bought a mobile home up north and spent a lot of time there. During the winter for several years we went to Florida.

Before we retired we knew what our income was going to be. We knew that we could not make any big purchases at that time because our pension was very small. We are in better shape now because we get Social Security.

My wife talked about retiring; she was more in favor of it than I was. She was enthusiastic about my taking the 30 and out. She retired at the end of the school year in June, and I retired in October when I had my 30 years in.

I enjoy retirement; the only thing is I have had a few medical problems, but I guess everybody had something at 65. I had a stroke eight years ago and it left me somewhat impaired. We sold our home up north because it was just too much work having two places.

We have lived in our house for 38 years and haven't thought about moving into a retirement community. As long as our health remains fair and we can do the necessary jobs around the house, we plan on staying here.

Since we retired we do the same things as before. We get up in the morning, have breakfast, eat lunch, then maybe we'll go shopping during the day; Sundays are for church and Bible class.

My wife enjoys retirement. I think she wants me home; she wants both of us home. It's nice to get up in the morning when you don't have an alarm clock to set, and do what you want to do.

THE "30 AND OUT" RETIREMENT OPTION

Pension programs were initiated in the automobile industry in 1951 by negotiations between the United Auto Workers and the Ford Motor Company. Prior to that time, according to Douglas Fraser, former U.A.W. president, "people were disabled or died before they left the job" (Institute of Gerontology, 1988).

Labor-management pension plans have evolved with many changes through the years: implementation by other industries, the inclusion of white-collar workers, increased pension monies, and health and insurance benefits. In 1973 the "30 and out" option was agreed to by the automobile companies and unions. This provision allowed workers to voluntarily retire based on their age and years of service.

The conversation of this retiree, who retired at the age of 53—nine years before he would qualify for even the reduced 20 percent of Social Security income, suggests some reasons why workers elect early retirement.

He started his job with an automobile company at 23. Thirty years later, although he enjoyed his work, he felt the fatigue of his labor and was somewhat overwhelmed with the increasing complexity of his job. These factors, combined with his wife's desire for both of them to retire and the availability of the "30 and out" option, made his decision acceptable and desired. He recognized and accepted a basic objective of his union: older workers retiring to make room for younger workers to get jobs.

9

Rabbinical Retirement

Male, 72, married, three children

Education:	college graduate
Job Status:	rabbi, for 45 years
Retirement Income:	$35,000
Health:	reported good
Retirement Category:	regular-voluntary, retired for 6 years, present status: rabbi emeritus

I was always interested in being a rabbi, the best that I could possibly be. The work was meaningful, interesting, never a dull day, never two days alike. I felt that it was a devotion and a dedication to my work, to my people.

I thought about retirement 10 to 12 years before I actually retired. This planning was part of my interest to continue teaching at a local university, where I served as an adjunct professor for 12 years before I retired. I have always believed that one plans one's retirement many years in advance; I have impressed this point on others who are in the same boat.

The only worry I had about retirement while I was working concerned finances. I knew that once I retired my income would be less; there would be less opportunity for augmenting my income. I needed to feel confident that my income would be sufficient to cover my needs so that I could retire with dignity and live in the manner to which I had become accustomed.

I never thought about early retirement because my arrangements with the rabbinical pension board were predicated on my retiring at age 65.

I had little time for friends or family while I was working. The job was 8 days and 8 nights every week. I never took a day off; the only time when I was not available was when I was out of town. I looked forward every month or six weeks to go to an out-of-state meeting for a change of faces, a change of pace. But I was always available for life-threatening matters.

It seemed to me one of the major decisions to be made about retirement was where do you want to live? Do you wish to remain in the city where you've worked for so many years, or move to the Sunbelt: Arizona, California or Florida. There are pros and cons of retiring in the area where you have worked as a minister, rabbi, or priest. The question is whether you wish to remain in your community among your people, be accessible and available to them even though retired, or move and cut your ties completely. I have friends who have followed both courses.

My wife and I decided to remain here to be available to members of our congregation and our friends and family, as well as continue my teaching activities at the university. This academic association has been meaningful to me through the years: I enjoyed the intellectual stimulation. The university world is very different from the congregational world.

It might be a good idea for me to explain what retirement means for a rabbi and what the emeritus status signifies. There are various kinds of emeritus rabbis. One moves away and completely cuts his ties with his city, congregation and the community. I chose a different kind of retirement, continuing my involvement with the congregation. As rabbi emeritus, I am permitted to officiate at life cycle events, officiating at weddings, funerals and the like. Also, any income that I would be able to obtain would be in addition to my pension. This honoraria, for officiation at these various events, became an important part of my income. Also, I functioned as my temple's ambassador-at-large in terms of serving on various boards of Jewish and non-Jewish agencies and organizations around the country.

The congregation provided an office and secretarial assistance for me. The big change when I became rabbi emeritus was that I was no longer responsible for the services, for preaching, for the administration of the congregation. I had no deadlines, no responsibilities; I was free.

A magnificent farewell service climaxed my retirement. A number of my friends in the congregation and the community spoke, and I felt it was a beautiful and greatly appreciated tribute.

Three things happened the day I retired, all by coincidence. All details for my retirement were completed and signed, the university where I teach confirmed the arrangement for an endowed chair to be established in my honor, and my wife got a job managing a large apartment complex.

My daily pattern now is to go to my office every day for a couple of hours, receive mail, messages. Now I have more time to have lunch with my wife.

I have been involved with retirement matters, other than my own plans, through the years. I participated in several seminars of a national organization and helped form a new group specifically dedicated to assist rabbis plan for their retirement. We meet annually to try to be of help to each other in retirement. I had a call recently from a rabbi, 68 years old, who had led his congregation for 30 years, who was thinking of retiring. He wondered how does one go about retiring . . . what are some of the arrangements . . . whom do you counsel with. He had made no arrangements. I said that I would be available to him.

Two years ago I was called back to active duty again due to some internal problems. For about a year it was again a full-time job, eight days a week. The weekends were especially trying because there were Friday night services, Saturday morning services, weddings Saturday night, funerals Sunday morning and afternoon or evening, condolence calls and hospital calls to make. Monday morning it started all over again with counseling, meetings, getting the bulletin out, writing articles, perparing sermons. It was a stressful time and for the most part I did not have an assistant.

When I was called back after six years I had forgotten how much I had been involved in running the congregation, but it was much easier the second time around because of my experience. This time everything I did was appreciated; I had the full support of the board. Before I retired the waters were never calm, there was always division and criticism; this time people realized that I was needed, and as they said, I was an answer to their prayers.

My wife likes the idea that I retired. As the rabbi's wife she was under some pressure to attend many types of functions. She did her part graciously, but she is relieved; now that I've retired, she feels she has retired from the congregation. Now she has the opportunity to handle this apartment complex job on a half-time basis.

My advice about retirement is to plan early; I would say five to ten years ahead of time. This planning should involve what you are going to do with your time, and of course, financial planning is necessary for everyone. Where you are going to live—in your hometown or seek a retirement community in the Sunbelt—is another subject to address before you retire.

RABBINICAL RETIREMENT

The issues many of us think about before we retire are often similar: income, use of our time, living arrangements, freedom, reduced pressure and responsibilities. We are in reasonable agreement about these subjects since it is clear retirement means a total break from all aspects of our former job. Those in religious service, due to the personal nature of their profession, are faced with similar issues regarding their retirement, but must also come to terms with their decision regarding continued involvement with their congregation.

The retirement of this rabbi, after some 45 years of service, provides a view of his future options. Further, it gives some definition to the time demands and the pressures of serving in a religious body. Perhaps it is taken for granted that those who elect the profession of religious leadership have made their independent decision to serve. However, what may not be understood is that their religious commitment excludes any personal time.

The work pattern, described for his eight-day week with little time for family and friends, suggests why he welcomed the idea of retirement. The resolution of his retirement income, with the opportunity to continue his teaching activity at a local university, formed the basis for electing the emeritus status, thereby maintaining some relationship with his congregation.

Two points of future life planning emphasized by this retiree, namely timeliness of planning and living arrangements, are worthwhile to consider. His suggestion of five to ten years of advanced planning provides an opportunity to think about possible changes in the future—in income and activities. Some knowledge and appreciation of your lifestyle will contribute to your transition to retirement.

10

Early Retirement Offers

Whatever the basis for your decision to retire, the increase in early retirement offered by employers is worth reviewing in view of business consolidations and large-scale personnel reductions.

Suppose your boss came to you one day and said, "We are going to offer you early retirement." How would you react?

Early retirement offers vary as to the specifics, but often consist of a flat amount of money or a percentage of one's regular salary to the age of 65.

Most early retirement offers are sudden and unexpected. Although the decision to accept or decline appears voluntary on the part of the employee, often the reality is that there will be a change in job status. If the employee declines the company's proposition, he or she may expect the loss of their job or a demotion in work grade and income.

The concerns of workers who receive offers of early retirement leave little doubt as to their feelings and attitudes to this sudden turn of events. While many people state they look forward to early retirement prior to age 65, they have not been confronted with the fact by their employer. On one hand, the employee views the option of retiring early as desirable, a time of life without the burden of work, but when the choice of working or retiring is removed and decided by the employer, all real and imagined concerns come to the surface.

Would you be prepared if you received an early retirement offer? Do you have confidence about the future in getting another full- or part-time job, or accepting retirement?

These are now important subjects for you to consider. First, the question of finances, your present, often soon-to-be-reduced income, and your lifestyle are primary considerations. Have you engaged in specific financial planning for the future? Do you have accurate figures as to your income and expenses?

Generally, people who work have a reasonable idea about their financial affairs. The assumption is they will spend less when they retire. One retiree who had neglected the area of financial planning stated, "I was surprised to discover when I retired that I had more time to spend money."

Many retirees who have planned their finances through the years nevertheless feel at loose ends when they receive early retirement. Their work patterns have been an integral part of their lives for many years. Now what was their role in life? The idea of filling time totally away from some kind of employment was disruptive. Further, many had made no plans for retirement, had no hobbies or interests other than their work.

After the initial shock of receiving an early retirement offer, some retirees are optimistic about their future. They are confident about securing other employment on a reduced basis so that the combined income from their former employer and the new job would reduce any financial strain.

What can be learned from the early retirement experience of others? Regardless of your present type of job, even at a high corporate level or income, you might be faced with early retirement. If you have not come to terms with this possibility because you feel secure in your present job, consider the increase in employer-mandated early retirement options.

Future planning now in matters of finances, use of your time, job possibilities and other retirement-related subjects will assist you in avoiding frustration and the trauma of being presented with an early retirement offer.

11

Retirement Blues

Whatever the nature of your decision about retirement activities, it should be a personal one founded on your particular areas of pleasure and fulfillment. These decisions, for some people, are not made immediately; often a transition period takes place which may be pleasant or painful. This transition involves both fact and feeling. The fact that you are no longer employed is self-evident, but your feelings about it all may prove to be much more difficult to get a handle on. If you wake one morning, feeling listless, puzzled by the lack of desire to do almost anything, you may very well be in the clutches of the retirement blues.

If retirement blues are one of your problems when you leave the world of work, be comforted—we have all experienced them in one form or another. But during your working years, the cause of depression was less obscure—job stress, family arguments, problems with the kids, bills, and so forth. The difference now is that you are confused; you cannot think of any particular reason for your state of mind.

One thing is certain: You are experiencing many changes when you retire. A change in hours and schedule is unavoidable. Perhaps you are suffering from your previous "time binding," when you were chained to time (Suinn, 1976). You are looking at different faces, the conversation is not work related, and possibly this is the first time in your life when the daily pressure and stress is gone.

Dr. R. H. Hirschowitz of Harvard Medical School suggests one reason for your feelings. He states: "It is axiomatic that all changes involve loss. Whenever men give up their attachment to familiar places, people, habits, routines and ways of seeing and doing, they feel a very real sense of loss. Even when change is attractive and desired, some sense of loss is inevitable" (Hirschowitz, 1974).

If you looked forward to retirement, it may appear difficult to realize you are feeling a sense of loss. Your daily pattern, although anticipated, is different and will take some patience on your part to accept and adjust to.

My own experience with retirement blues is an example of personal dislocation. For a while I was confused by my lack of interest and motivation. I considered the matter and realized I had no structure in my life. I came to understand that structure of some sort, to some degree—not necessarily every day—was required for my healthy mental balance. So the volunteer activity, the continued effort to talk to men and women who had retired, brought me again into some focus of life around me.

I suggest that you not be too hard on yourself. If possible, attempt to think through some of the events that preceded your depressed feelings. One of the best methods to understand your situation is to talk to someone—someone who listens. This may be a difficult task since few have the capacity to listen—everyone wants to talk.

The person you tell your story to might be another retiree. Often someone who has shared some of the same confusion and bewilderment knows the source of your problem. Whether their particular experience mirrors yours or not is not important, but the strategies they employed to find peace and meaning during their retired years will prove invaluable.

When you are at your bluest, remember you are one of the survivors. You have had your successes and failures in the job market. You have carried the role of family member, in whatever capacity, with tears and laughter throughout the years. And the many years of your life have provided you with a great understanding of yourself and the world around you.

Now you have a job to do—to find yourself, to discover the meaning of life in this new atmosphere, unencumbered by both the pressures and pleasures of the job. You now have the power and the ability to select the time and the place for whatever it is you need or desire to do. There is no question, with the unfettered time you now possess, that you have the capacity to find your way through this temporary maze—your unmarked journey on the way to a satisfying retirement.

II

WORK VERSUS RETIREMENT

" . . . I sometimes missed working . . . "
" . . . each promotion represented a challenge . . . "
"This left a tremendous void in my life . . . "
"I had made my major contribution . . . "
"I was coming to a different point in my life . . . "
"was on the edge of burnout . . . "

12

The Meaning of Work and Retirement

What has your work meant to you? What satisfactions did your work provide? Was your social identity established by your work role? These questions are addressed because they bear directly on how some people make the adjustment to retirement.

Most of us do not consciously think on a daily basis of the meaning of work while we are employed. Such matters as income, whether or not the work is interesting, our relationships with others on the job, and the satisfactions we receive are often taken for granted. But with the event of retirement, either voluntary or mandatory, the change from the work to the retired role may produce contrasting feelings of relief and regret, anticipation and anxiety. The structure that work offers, as well as the identity of the job role, provides a foundation from which a person functions and views himself or herself.

The impact of retirement for the men and women in this section provides some insight into the influence of work on their patterns of retirement.

Three patterns are presented. The first, satisfaction with total retirement . . . a high school principal who accepted the fact that it was time for a change and who made the required effort to remain involved in a life-style similar to his career . . . a social worker who accepted the role of retiree as but another step in her life.

The second pattern, a combination of available options combined with some part-time work . . . a librarian who found balance in her life by returning to part-time work . . . a minister who realized pleasure in retirement on the basis of part-time activity in his chosen field.

Our third illustration of the work-retirement relationship represents some regret and disorientation to the event . . . a corporate president who accepted mandatory retirement at 65, enjoyed post-retirement activities but acknowledged his longing for his former work-related friendships . . . an acknowledged workaholic who became depressed because his lifetime focus was work.

What our work means to us, in its many dimensions, is important to consider when we think of retirement. Generally, people who find some of the same gratifications and meaning in their retirement that work formerly provided will be on the way to adjusting more satisfactorily in their new role of retiree.

The adjustments many people are confronted with in retirement include financial matters, use of time, relationships with spouse and family, and changes in vitality and health. But as important as anything else in considering and accepting retirement is how we feel about ourselves.

Our feelings and attitudes in this new non-work role will depend in some measure on how we felt about our work. If our job had little meaning outside of the paycheck, the pressure and stress of the past will not be missed. If, however, our work was a source of personal satisfaction and contributed to our sense of self-worth, it is important to think about activities in retirement which are similar in their personal fulfillment.

The relationship of our retirement activities and adjustment is suggested by the following: "Case studies of patterns of successful and unsuccessful retirement show the variety of activities that might be enjoyed. But the picture which emerges indicates that it is not the activities themselves but the meaning which the individual is able to give to the activities which determines his adjustment" (Back, 1969).

13

Conflict of Work and Retirement

Female, 64, married, four children

Education:	college graduate
Job Status:	librarian, for 22 years
Retirement Income:	$20,000
Health:	reported good
Retirement Category:	early-voluntary, retired for 4 years, returned to part-time work

I enjoyed my work thoroughly. It was a main interest in my life, but not my only interest. I always felt I could have done better if I had been willing to change libraries or change jobs. It was comfortable staying where I was in terms of my life; it's easier not to make changes than to change. If I took another job out of town, that would have required my husband's relocation, and that was out of the question.

I never looked forward to retirement. I thought about it as something in the future, but something happened in our lives that made me realize I should retire because of my husband's illness. I was very concerned about his health, how much longer he would live. I felt because he was retired it was selfish for me not to retire and spend this time with him. I was concerned about making him happy in what I thought were the last years of his life.

My work at the time was exciting. We were reorganizing the department; I was training other people to do the various jobs. I was so engaged with my working life that I felt retirement was far in the future.

Working took a lot of my energy. We led a fairly quiet life. We had a few close friends that we went to dinner with and to the theatre and some concerts. I didn't have time for any volunteer activities or women's groups or card games.

I hardly thought about retirement, but most of the people I was friendly with who had retired would always come back and tell us how happy they were. For that reason, I thought about it in positive terms as a time to explore new interests, or to travel, or to lead a good life in general.

We didn't do any retirement planning. We've kept our wills up to date, but not in terms of retirement. It was a matter of estate planning and tax avoidance for the kids. I always thought I would retire to Florida. My husband's parents had retired there and I liked the area. In the back of my mind I thought, "Well, if I retire, we'll spend more time in Florida—instead of a week, maybe a month or two."

Before I retired, we found a vacation spot in California that we enjoyed, but we never spent more than two weeks there. The first year after I retired we rented a home in that area for three months. The idea was to explore whether I would like it there. We had no intention of buying, but merely to rent for the three months of winter. On the last day we impulsively bought the home. That summer I suffered "buyer's remorse." But when we returned to our new home, I was very happy. By the second day I knew we had done the right thing.

About the time of my retirement I investigated some classes on retirement planning offered by the city for library personnel. They told me they were booked for that year, which was fine with me. I felt I was in enough control of my life, and my husband was informed financially. We have always been very conservative; our policy is never to borrow money or pay for anything on time. If I want something, we save for it; if we can't pay cash we don't buy it.

My husband was pleased with my decision to retire. He had liquidated his business and been retired for 3 or 4 years off and on, with some years as a real estate salesman and stockbroker, all of which he disliked. He had never worked for other people, so it was a difficult situation for him.

In a general way I knew something about our finances. I would get my pension and start collecting Social Security in a couple of years along with my husband. We had some investments, and while the income does vary, my husband is informed of these matters and we knew our lifestyle would go on. We wouldn't be able to do glamorous things, like a trip around the world. We both knew if we had to lower our standard of living we could manage. We could always sell our house and move to simpler accommodations.

I was a little fearful whether I would be busy enough when I retired. I've always been a busy person—never been bored. I've always found things that made me happy. I hoped, even though I didn't know what those activities were going to be, that I would find them again.

During the first year I sometimes missed working and being with the people I had become close to for 20 years. I felt like I wasn't doing anything useful to the world.

When I retired for the first summer, I signed up for a million activities. I programmed myself really crazy and I realized what I was doing. I had every day filled as though I had to go to work every day, even though they were supposed to be leisure activities. I calmed down after that summer was over and tried to schedule myself with some common sense.

I would say to others, know yourself, don't try to do things other people might expect of you; do things that you like. This is your time to explore. Your children are grown, your responsibilities are lessened, so this is your opportunity for many options. I am fortunate in not having to worry about economic problems—finances and health problems would be a burden in retirement.

Sometimes I missed my work. I can see that when you wake up in the morning you always know where you are going and what you are going to do. Once in a while I feel it's hard being retired. It's almost more work than it's worth, deciding what to do, making the phone calls to find other people to share some activity. These were all the things I never had to do when I was working. I had so little free time that I knew exactly what I was going to do with it—do things with my friends or take care of my household activities.

I assume that most people do plan for their retirement. In my case it just sort of flowed into my life without any planning.

During the second year after my retirement, I was called by the library people about a particular problem they were having. They wondered if I could provide some assistance. I listened to the work that was offered; I was very interested. I told them I would be returning to California. They agreed—I would work as a consultant and be paid by the hour. I would determine the hours I worked.

I enjoy the work, like getting the money and working with the people I had missed for the past couple of years. I imagine I was a little flattered; this was the first time a retiree had ever been brought back to work.

I like my life here better than the one I led in California. Here I am busier, closer to my longtime friends, and I'm vocationally involved. For me, interesting work keeps my brain involved. It's like solving puzzles—something I've always enjoyed. I know I like activity, places to go, and so I plan to start my volunteer activity again. This time I will not over-program myself.

WILL YOUR RETIREMENT BE A STRUGGLE BETWEEN WORK AND LEISURE?

Your voluntary decision to retire, unless health is the major reason, will be based on some expectation that your daily living will be more pleasurable and satisfying than working. Total retirement is not an acceptable alternative for some men and women because they have failed to find sufficient substitutes for what their job provided. The conversation of this retiree, who found her work of 22 years and the related associations satisfying, is an example of a tug-of-war between work and retirement.

This retirement decision was made because of her husband's life-threatening illness; retirement was viewed as "something in the future." She felt drawn in two directions: the devotion for her husband, and the exciting nature of her work. This ambivalence resulted in a fear of being insufficiently occupied in retirement. She realized that what she was doing in over-programming her activities during the first year was a futile attempt to compensate for her former daily work pattern.

The description of her retirement, "it's almost more work than it's worth"—deciding on activities and finding others to share these inter-ests—provides a picture of the lack of fulfillment she experienced. This frustration, combined with a perception she was not doing anything useful, and continuing to miss the meaning of what her work had provided after two years of retirement, illustrates her struggle.

The request for her to return to work on a part-time basis during the summer months appears to have provided a satisfactory solution. Now, in her home setting, occupied with challenging work and the joy of working with her friends in the library setting, she has attained some balance in her life.

The message this retirement episode suggests is that for some a mixture of meaningful work activity and the leisure of retirement are necessary ingredients to appreciate the significance of one's life.

14

The Friendship of Fellow Workers

Male, 82, married, three children

Education:	high school graduate
Job Status:	corporation CEO, 44 years with major international corporation
Retirement Income:	$200,000
Health:	reported good
Retirement Category:	regular-mandatory, retired for 16 years

When I started with my company, some sixty years ago, my job was at the bottom of the ladder. During the course of my career I held many positions and each promotion represented a challenge, a new opportunity, and as a result I enjoyed every assignment.

Retirement was something that I wanted to avoid as long as possible. Age 65 was mandatory retirement at my company, as it was with many other corporations as a result of the Social Security provision. I think a lot of people, at the upper corporate level, could have worked beyond 65; their health and mental capacity were good enough to allow them to continue working, but there still had to be an opportunity for the younger people coming along. If everybody had his own option with respect to retirement, it would create such a roadblock that it would be an impossible situation.

I never worried about retirement; I knew that there was something I could do to occupy my time. I was fully occupied right up to the last minute of my active responsibility.

My health had been excellent through the years, even with the long hours I put in. I left the house at seven o'clock in the morning and returned at seven-thirty at night; there was always work to do over the weekends.

I never understood the attitude of so many people just waiting to retire. The U.A.W. had this "30 and out" retirement policy and many people took advantage of it. That was all they looked forward to for the last five or six years of their working experience. Frankly, I never understood that attitude because I enjoyed my work.

My activities, other than work, were very few. I tried golf for a while but gave that up because I didn't have enough time. I loved to fish, but I didn't have as much opportunity as I would have liked. I had no hobbies because the responsibilities of my job were full time.

We had a lot of social things to go to in different parts of the country, which I considered part of my job. We really had no close friends.

I looked at retirement as an entirely different life, a slower-paced life, a life of more leisure and an opportunity to do things that I hadn't been able to do before, including traveling. I traveled extensively as part of my career, but really never had time to see anything. When I retired we made several trips in this country and Europe to see a few of the things we had missed.

Generally, I have been a planner through the years on personal affairs, my job schedules, and fortunately, I have been busy enough in my retirement that it always required planning. But frankly, because I was so busy in my job and the idea of planning for retirement was not intriguing, I did not engage in any specific planning for my retirement. As a prudent person, I have tried over the years to manage my financial affairs, but not with the specific idea related to retiring.

We bought a condominium down South about a year after I retired. The idea was to get away from the northern winters and visit with relatives in that area.

I did not look forward to retirement. I regretted the necessity of leaving the daily association with people with whom I had worked for so many years. I was fortunate, shortly before I retired, to receive a number of different offers of directorships and other assignments, so I could pick and choose.

There really wasn't anything to discuss with my wife about my retirement since it was mandatory. We were going to stay in our house that we had lived in for over 30 years and enjoy the winters down South.

Along with my work on the boards of directors of some major American corporations, I got a call from Washington to head a committee related to our military service. I had an office in Washington and spent seven years commuting to this job. This work was interesting; it required extensive travel. I met some fine people and had an opportunity to become acquainted with the Washington scene.

I don't think in any sense of the word that I got the satisfaction out of these retirement activities that I had derived from my business career. It seems to me, if you have your health, you can find some interest to keep you active. If you don't have reasonably good health, everything goes by the board. I think I made the most of the opportunities available to me in retirement and I enjoyed what I was doing, but in no way was it as good as working.

As far as our married life is concerned, I've had a very understanding wife. She put up with all of my traveling and had the burden of raising the kids when they were young because I was gone so much of the time. Now in retirement she has her friends and leads much the same kind of life she led while I was working. I have many things to do, a lot of reading, and traveling connected with my board of director positions. We have been married over 50 years and know each other pretty well by this time.

I think the average person should do a lot of financial planning; seek the counsel of a bank or some responsible institution. This is essential. I was fortunate in having little in the way of financial concerns; I knew what my retirement income would be from my former employer and what my assets were. It is important to include insurance in financial planning because, with today's medical costs, it is vital to be properly covered.

THE INFLUENCE OF WORK ASSOCIATES ON RETIREMENT

One of the concerns some people express when they think about retirement is that they would miss their friends at work. Such considerations as retirement income and the state of their health are prime areas immediately confronted by men and women when they retire. The subtle influence, however, of relationships developed on the job over many years is significant in one's satisfactory adjustment to retirement.

The conversation of this retiree, who wanted to avoid retirement but accepted his corporation's mandatory decision at age 65, poses some questions as to why he failed to get satisfaction "out of these retirement activities that I had derived from my business career." As he stated, he was fortunate in having the opportunity to select various offers of corporate directorships as well as a federal government assignment in

Washington. These activities were interesting—enjoyable—"but in no way was it as good as working."

What was missing? Were the perks, the power, the work itself the missing ingredients that he found so enjoyable when he was working?

I contacted this retiree for some explanation of what was lacking in his retirement experience that was so rewarding during his years of employment. He stated that it was not the work, nor the supposed power of a CEO, but the people: "I made many friends in all levels of the corporation and after some fifty years I missed these relationships."

The prestige of corporate leaders, their activities and their financial power and recompense, is something few of us will ever know anything about. However, the conversation of this retiree, who enjoyed the challenges of his work career, presents a picture of the demands of upper corporate jobs.

His mandatory retirement at age 65, by corporate requirement, was not a decision of his choice. His weekly work schedule required an almost 12-hour day plus weekend work. There was little time or opportunity for avocational interests because, as he stated, "the responsibilities of my job were full time." He had developed no close friendships, outside of his business associates, due to the extent of his business obligations.

When you consider this man's devotion to his job, combined with the almost total time requirement, it is clear some loss would be felt when he retired. He was to recall with some regret leaving a job where meaningful friendships were a thing of the past.

15

Problems of a Workaholic

Male, 68, married, two children

Education:	high school graduate
Job Status:	owner, building supplies for 50 years
Retirement Income:	$250,000
Health:	reported good
Retirement Category:	regular-voluntary, retired for four years

I was a workaholic. I worked seven days and nights. Even on Sundays and holidays I would bring home a briefcase of work and start again after dinner.

My company was at the top of the heap. We were successful in everybody's eyes, including the bank's eyes, so I had the pride of accomplishment.

We had a wonderful organization, like one family. We always gave generous bonuses at Christmastime, because my attitude was life is a two-way street and these people had been instrumental in our success.

I had looked forward to semiretirement. My daughter married a young man whom I brought into our company and taught our business. After a year he seemed to have the right attitude; he was able to assume some of my responsibilities. My plan was to move to our condominium in Florida, where the grandchildren could visit, and every couple of weeks I would fly back to oversee my operation.

I have always been a great believer in people, and with the proper key people we could have expanded our business. I never believed in full retirement; my idea was that I could be semiretired with key people.

The business climate changed and about the same time my son-in-law said to my daughter that he wanted space, so they got a divorce. I told him to turn in his credit cards, keys to his cars, and walk. Everything seemed to be cascading on me in the early '80s—the poor economy, my daughter's divorce and my becoming 65. It was devastating; it knocked me for a loop. In fact, to be very candid with you, I am just beginning to feel myself again. It has taken almost four years.

I had never dreamed of being retired. Through the years I had planned only from a business standpoint. Thank God my wife and kids were healthy and I had come through heart surgery very successfully about five years ago, so I never thought about my health. I knew I was the cock-of-the-walk in my industry and I let everyone know it. Then the bottom fell out of all my dreams, all my plans.

When I realized that I had to close the business and retire, the economy was poor. We had considerable sums of money in accounts receivable and a huge inventory. I spent most of my time settling these accounts and liquidating the inventory. But my life was completely changed now. For 50 years I had gotten up in the morning and I never had to worry about where I was going or what I was going to do. I always had plans . . . who I was going to see, who to call . . . and what jobs we were starting. I never planned on what I was going to do tomorrow; my days had always been the same. This left a tremendous void in my life when I finally realized my business days were over.

When the business was operating I always had 10 or 12 office personnel around me. There were people to talk to, people to see; there was always something going on. Then, when the doors were closed on my business, I would sit in my office alone, with no one around, no one calling me. I had nobody to call. I had money, but I didn't know what to do. I had no plans. I wanted to run.

I think part of my feeling came from the fact that I was a Depression baby. I remember when a neighbor lady came over to borrow a dollar from my mother, who had to refuse her because my father only had one dollar in his pocket. These times made an indelible imprint on my mind.

I have felt somewhat better about things in the last year or so. I resented retiring. I was envious of those who stayed in the business, especially since the economy bounced back. My doctor thought I had been going through a period of depression. I don't know if he was right, but I was low, really down, and this was something for a guy who had been the cock-of-the-walk in his industry. All of a sudden, I was nothing, just like Joe Blow out on the street, with no place to go.

I had an uncle who had retired while I was still in business who used to walk in unannounced and visit. He would take his coat off, sit at our big conference table and talk. I was usually busy, but we would talk about insignificant things, trivia. After a while, I would hit the desk and say, "Okay, Uncle, I have to go to work." He would pick himself up and leave, not angry. I could never see myself doing anything like that with my friends. I am not that kind of a person. I was strictly business.

I still find living difficult, but I am making an effort. I have rejoined a golf club and am getting more involved with some old friends and new acquaintances. I may be getting back into a business venture, which will really have me busy again.

I tell my son and son-in-law, "Find hobbies, something that will keep you interested; get diversified." Someone gave me this advice, but I pooh-poohed it, I didn't listen. I think a man should, while he is going and growing and making money, be smart enough to say, "Hey, I can't do this forever; I had better have some other avenues to keep my time occupied."

I have tried fishing, golf, playing cards and walking. But I have to have something tangible, something to make me feel creative. Yesterday I visited a plant. When I saw all the activity going on, I felt like a boy again. I had been in construction over 50 years and when I heard the sound of saws again I felt young. That really turned me on. I want to get into something creative, something where I will be mentally involved.

My wife has been very understanding while all this was going on. She did resent my being busy all the time and not spending more time with her and the children. My argument was that I could not have made what I did by spending time at home.

Life is strange as far as who you marry, both for men and women. I married a gal who does not share any of my interests, nor do I share any of hers. I love sports, which are of no interest to her. She loves dancing, and I didn't have time for dancing. She likes to play cards; this is not my cup of tea. I like to walk; she doesn't like this exercise. I guess opposites attract.

As far as any advice I could give to others, I would say avoid retirement. The big thing is to keep your head going. I don't have to work another day of my life if my investments are solid, but this is not enough. A person should think of different things to do, have ideas how to benefit oneself and family and the community.

CAN A WORKAHOLIC FIND MEANING IN RETIREMENT?

Is there more to life than work? This question is affirmatively answered by a growing number of workers who are retiring at age 65 or earlier. These decisions to retire are made in the face of general work satisfaction, but a view of the days without job tension, routine and responsibility beckon to the world of freedom and other options in one's life. Whether the worker who looks forward to retirement finds joy, pleasure and satisfaction in his or her life without the constraints of work remains an individual affair.

The conversation of this retiree brings to the surface many reasons for his rejection of retirement.

His statement that "I was a Depression baby" might well be a significant reason for his rejection of retirement. His generation, which struggled to survive during the Great Depression, will carry some part of those dark days with them forever. The economic success that he had realized through the years was evidently an insufficient reason for him to stop working.

This man's almost total devotion to his work, with little time or attention paid to his family, had developed a pattern that was difficult to alter.

The excitement of the work scene, the feeling of fulfillment from creative activity combined with the satisfaction of success, "I knew I was the cock-of-the-walk in my industry," resulted in his depression when his business closed.

This coming together of early background experiences, the satisfaction of success, the lack of family involvement and some resentment of the aging process all suggest he will continue to heed the call to work.

16

Part-Time
Work—Transition to
Retirement

Male, 70, married, one child

Education:	college graduate
Job Status:	high school principal, 42 years in education
Retirement Income:	$25,000
Health:	reported good
Retirement Category:	regular-mandatory, retired for five years

I enjoyed my career; it was interesting and meaningful. The most challenging part of it was the last three years.

I don't think I looked forward to retirement. I didn't know how I was going to react to it. My wife kept saying through the years that I needed to develop some hobbies that could be pursued after retirement. Frankly, I had few. I can't say that I was looking forward to retirement, because I was enjoying my work. But now I am almost as busy as when I was working.

If there was any part of my career that I wasn't enjoying fully, it was the last three to five years. It was the time when there was quite a revolt on the part of young people as to standard ways of doing things, and it was frustrating. We went through several student demonstrations. I don't think we ever had the degree of student revolt that was experienced in some communities, but we did have demonstrations, and a few instances of marches and parades. These were upsetting to the general routine of operation. We found ourselves in the position of having to change a lot of our policies; our policy on dress codes, and even the matter of discipline became a matter that had to be handled in a different way. I set up a number of student faculty committees to work out policies and procedures to be followed, which were big changes from what we had previously. At no time, however, was the degree of student demonstrations and that sort of thing to the point where it closed our schools.

The only health problem that I had was in the last year before I retired. I suffered a mild heart attack, which did limit my activities. Since that time my health has been good.

Before I retired, I was very active in a number of organizations—civic affairs, Rotary Club and my church. I was also a member of the state athletic commission and was very active in the development of interscholastic athletic programs for the state. I served on the accreditation agency for high schools and universities in this part of the country.

Due to my school and outside activities, my time was somewhat limited as far as being able to see and enjoy the company of my friends. I had a lot of evening meetings, and so we associated with our friends pretty much over the weekends. As far as my family was concerned, since I live right here in town, it made it possible for me to go home for dinner and then still have time for the meetings in the evening.

I think I would have to be honest and say that I didn't give retirement a lot of thought. I knew it was something out there that I was eventually going to have to face. I suppose one of the main reasons for this is that I was so involved with my work most of my life.

Due to the fact that the last three years of my active career were less satisfying than the previous ones, retirement was accepted a little more graciously than it would have been three years earlier. I had gotten to the point where I was somewhat glad to be getting out of the routine. I felt that perhaps I had made my major contribution and it was time for a change.

My major concern had to do with activities to keep me occupied. I had been an active, busy person and I couldn't see myself just doing anything. This is one of the reasons that I took on a part-time job for the university as a consultant. It was a transitional period and it gave me some structure. I wasn't retired very long until I found plenty to do.

My wife and I discussed retirement a number of times. We were both committed to the idea that we wanted to remain here where I had worked. We had lived in this town for so many years and our roots are deep. I have always had the feeling that I never wanted to go off to a distant place somewhere to retire. I've got friends here, which would makeiteasier to establish routines and new activities than it would be in an entirely new situation.

My wife was mainly concerned about whether or not I would find opportunities to keep me occupied. I think that was her greatest concern.

Before I retired, I had a pretty good idea of what our total income would be. I had worked this out with the retirement office, and made a number of trips to determine what these monies were going to be. I felt that our general expenses would be less after I retired. Our plans have been to be able to live on income, and thus far we have.

When retirement became a fact, I accepted it, I was ready for it. Fortunately, the community had a retirement party for me, and that sort of paved the way. My wife and I were given a trip abroad as a retirement gift, so at the opening of school we were in England. This travel was the start of our retirement. When we came back from that trip, I started my part-time work at the local university for two winters, and at the same time I became involved in a lot of community activities. So things just fell into place.

I have been retired now for five years, and to tell the truth, I have enjoyed every minute of it. I have no regrets.

I have become involved in local civic affairs, joined a men's club, and this has sort of set up a schedule for me. I also served on a number of committees for the local board of education, and last year we developed a task force to explore the possibilities for the development of a program of community education. This, plus my activities on the church council, has resulted in a pretty full schedule, and it has been satisfying. I have had little time to wonder what I was going to do.

As far as any recommendations to others, the main thing, I don't think you can just sit and rock. From a health point of view, a person who has been active all his life can't just suddenly become inactive. You have to find activities to keep yourself engaged. I have always preferred not to go to a retirement area. First of all, I don't want to be associated solely with retired people. I associate with retired people, but I think it is good for my mental health to have associates who are not retired. I suppose when the day comes when my health doesn't permit me to be active, I will have to make adjustments. But I think you have to be an active person, you won't live very long if you're not occupied.

What I really like about retirement is that I have the opportunity to do things that I enjoy. I can say no to the things that I don't want to do, or don't feel qualified to do, or don't feel inclined to do. Being an old established person in the community, I have had an opportunity to choose. I think a person who might be retiring in a community in which he has not lived very long, or doesn't have deep roots, would be in a different situation. I have been able to pick and choose the things I want to do.

Since I retired, my income is less, but my expenses are also less. I think thus far it has worked out pretty much as we expected.

In my opinion, more thought and planning should be given to retirement. I was fortunate, due to the background of my job and my associations, that it was easier for me to adjust to retirement than it would have been for persons who have not had this background. People should do more planning. I think every person will have to find some areas of interest and develop activities for his retirement years. If you are interested in people, then you have to find ways to work with people. If you have hobbies that you can be comfortable with, that's fine. You have to find areas of interest that you can develop into ways of occupying your time. Of course, a very necessary part of planning is adequate financial planning so that you will be able to live a comfortable, productive life. There is a need to develop good habits to maintain your health, because the one thing that is basic to satisfactory retirement is health. Every person facing retirement has to arrive at some conclusion on where he wants to live. There are some people who are happiest going off to some retirement area to live, because they enjoy the kind of activities that would be involved there. I am not sure that I would be happy with that. Everyone has to determine where he wants to live and what he wants to do in the community.

These plans should be made well before retirement. I don't think you make them at the time of retirement. The average family educates its children and gets the responsibility of children taken care of probably by their early '50s, and once these responsibilities are taken care of, it is time to do some planning in terms of what you are going to do for retirement. This planning should start early.

CAN PART-TIME WORK ASSIST IN THE TRANSITION TO RETIREMENT?

The event of retirement for most people brings an end to their job-related activity. The impact is immediate, and the process of adjustment to retirement must be confronted. Where there are options of either continuing in the same line of work on a reduced basis, or some part-time effort in a second career activity, the transition to retirement is often eased. This retiree took advantage of the opportunity to maintain some contact in the field of education, while at the same time developing interests in the community which would provide the activity he sought.

This retiree's introduction to retirement, a gift from the community in the form of a trip to Europe, was a first step to a lifestyle without formal work after 24 years. Whether he would have missed the school opening is questionable in view of his general readiness to retire, but old patterns are not easily broken, and he was not faced with this immediate adjustment. He viewed his part-time consulting work at a local university for a year as a base from which he could examine what alternatives were available.

His continued involvement in community education, where his years of experience could be utilized, along with the local men's club and church activities, resulted in a workable pattern of living in retirement. This episode suggests that where it is possible to find a bridge between former job interests and the establishment of retirement activities, the anxiety of this life shift might be reduced.

17

A Change in Schedules

Female, 60, married, 3 children

Education: college graduate
Job Status: social work administrator for 14 years
Retirement Income: $25,000
Health: reported good
Retirement Category: early-voluntary, retired for two years

I fell into my job because I had been working as a volunteer in the field of emotionally disturbed children. I was asked to be the administrator of a new program to work with the schools to reach those children before they had to be separated from their homes. We developed a program for emotionally disturbed and abused children. The idea was to start meeting with families during pregnancy and be involved with them during the first year of the baby's life. We were really helping parents to become parents for the first time. We believed that if there is help for the family from the beginning and they make an attachment to the child, there will be no neglect or abuse.

Actually, I didn't have any particular feelings about retiring; I certainly was not afraid of quitting. I was coming to a different point in my life. I had been in volunteer work for 30 years, and after 14 years as a professional, I left the world of work two years ago.

Retirement for me is like heaven. When you're a kid, you have to deal with school and everything that goes with it. When I got married—three days after I graduated from college—I went to work. I could hardly wait to have children. When my husband started talking about retirement, I thought this is wonderful; he had done everything in his field of work.

He was a lawyer and he felt his work had become more of a business than a profession. My only concern for him was that he had never gone through a week without hearing from his clients or other attorneys and getting positive feedback. I didn't know whether he could drop these contacts and not feel the loss.

Retirement for me was an opportunity to experience coming together with my husband on an easy basis. If we wanted to take a trip, we wouldn't have to plan it for a weekend. If we wanted to pick up and go out to dinner, a movie, a play, we knew we had time without prior planning. I was never enthralled with a tight schedule, so the idea of having my own schedule again was terrific.

My husband has always been very open in terms of where we were moneywise. I had a roundabout idea about our income and we worked together on what our expenses would be.

I retired in May and my staff brought together 500 volunteers for a farewell party. It was a moving experience. Since we were going into summer, I knew that we were going up north to our cottage and stay a lot longer than we had been able to do in the past. We have two grandchildren and I wanted the freedom to see more of them without feeling pressured. I also have a mother in a nursing home, and I did not feel that I ever had enough time to be with her.

I knew I would never have any problem about how to spend my time, but I was concerned what retirement would be like for my husband. Once he made the decision to close his office, it took some months to accomplish it. He stopped taking clients, because when you take a client as a lawyer, his or her case might not come up for another two years, so he had to plan ahead. Naturally, his practice diminished and I wondered if he felt non-useful. He started doing a lot more reading and going to lunch with our son-in-law. I saw changes taking place long before he closed the office door. The changes were not hard on him. My only concern was that he would not feel adrift.

My husband likes his own company and he knows himself. He is very comfortable setting up his day as he wishes. Sometimes he lets it float. There are few people who can let a day float and not at one point or another wonder, "What am I doing?" or "What should I be doing?"

I think retirement is difficult work for a lot of people; for me it's just a change in schedule. It means that you still look around to do the kinds of things you want to do, to see what you want to see, experiment and find challenges in other ways; but the pace is different. For the first time in my life I am free.

There were no uncomfortable adjustments. The thing you find is that where you may have looked at your work as the reason for not doing some of the other things, now you have no excuse. So then you choose what you want to do, not because people are waiting for you. I suggest that people not be afraid to have time to explore. There is so much to do in this world that I think we become stultified, we are afraid to change our lives.

I think it is very important, whether you are retired or working, to see your friends on a regular basis. When I was working I had lunch with friends. My lunch was not a work hour. I've kept up with their lives because I was really interested in them. Getting together as a couple is different—just as delightful—but it's different. Getting together as two people, to be able to talk and have that basis when you retire, is important. You are going to end up with no one to connect with if the only people you were ever friends with were those at the job.

WILL YOUR OUTLOOK ON LIFE CHANGE IN RETIREMENT?

Retirement is defined by some scholars as: no full-time employment, minimum part-time employment and receiving monies from non-work sources, pensions and Social Security, and whether the persons consider themselves retired (Palmore, Burchett, Fillenbaum, George, & Wallman, 1985). It is often the personal definition and attitude one brings to retirement that predict satisfaction or stress in this life event.

The conversation of this retiree suggests her definition as a welcome "change of schedule." She recognized retirement as a shifting in her life from roles of schoolgirl, spouse, mother, worker, and now retiree. This period she views as an opportunity for a closer relationship with her husband and more time for family and friends. More important, perhaps, is her outlook that the future will continue to provide challenges to see, to do, to experience what life has to offer. Her attitude toward retirement suggests an enthusiastic redirection of interests and activities, along with a slower pace.

The importance of attitude is expressed by one leader in retirement education: "In a real sense, one's attitude about retirement can become a self-fulfilling prophecy; that is, the older person who looks forward to enjoying retirement is much more likely to enjoy it than someone who dreads it" (Atchely, 1976).

18

Value of Part-Time Work

Male, 64, married, five children

Education:	college graduate
Job Status:	Episcopalian rector for 41 years
Retirement Income:	$30,000
Health:	reported good
Retirement Category:	early-voluntary, retired for two years, occasional part-time work

My work involved being a parish minister in local churches. I've had four assignments in the past 41 years; my last church affiliation lasted over 23 years. I tended to be a workaholic because the work was so engrossing. It was stupid, but for the first years I never took a day off.

Retirement was something that I had looked forward to. Five years before I retired I had surgery for an abdominal aortic aneurysm, which was followed by a gallbladder operation. My energy level never snapped back to where it was before the surgery and since I felt that my parish would need vigorous leadership in the next five years, I decided to retire. I also looked forward to having the time to do some traveling and whatever else people do in retirement.

I really think I was on the edge of burnout by the time I retired. I consulted a psychologist, who suggested that I move to another job. Well, the realities of life at that point were that it was very hard to move—there were more clergymen than there were places for them to work.

As far as planning for retirement, I never gave it a thought as to what's going to happen. I wondered how was I going to live on what I was going to get when I retired. The people on our pension board were extremely helpful—they pointed out that I would have enough to live on and probably have a larger cash flow than I had ever seen in my life. My mother passed away and left me a small inheritance which, with the help of a local broker, has added to our income.

I was looking forward to retirement, but I realized that one of the things I could do was what we call "take service." What is involved here is take over for a clergyman who becomes ill; there is compensation for this service. Also there is a whole new thing called "interim minister." This is where the minister dies, and you take over for a short period until a replacement is found. I have provided service on this interim basis a few times for short periods.

My interests other than my work consisted of jogging, photography and meeting monthly with a group of clergy and their spouses for bridge. Four of our five children live reasonably close to our home, so we spend time with them.

I thought retirement was a kind of new beginning, not being tied to full-time parish administration, which I hated. The idea of taking service for other ministers looked like a challenge. We thought that retirement was an opportunity to travel to Florida and to England, where we have friends.

My wife is really the planner. I'm not good at that sort of thing. We talked about where we would live when I retired. We have one daughter who lives in the South and we investigated living near there. But with four of our kids living here who have children, it made sense to remain in this area.

When I made the decision to retire I had a great feeling of relief. I tell people it's the greatest invention since the wheel. It's not that it's problem-free. You will still have to determine how you are going to use your time. The freedom part comes from the fact that you made the decision, so the pressure and routine are things of the past.

Sometimes I think my wife has mixed feelings about my retirement. She was concerned about how she would keep me out of her hair with my offering suggestions on running the house. If I just sit around the house I'll drive her nuts—and myself. Now she is pleased that I work occasionally as an interim minister.

Planning for retirement I think is absolutely essential. You need to look at the economics. Where you are going to live is important to think about—and be careful about burning your bridges. One couple I knew sold their house here, moved to Florida and were back here within the year. From my perspective, retirement doesn't mean you stop being functional in terms of whatever you've been trained to do. I can't imagine not being involved somehow or other in worship and pastoral care.

If I had my life to live over, I would start thinking about retirement right at the beginning. It was our good fortune that when I decided to retire the numbers were right and we did not have to lower our standard of living. When you retire you have to decide what kind of life you are going to lead. You need to have a sense that when you stop working fulltime the significance of your life doesn't end.

WOULD YOU RETURN TO YOUR JOB ON A PART-TIME BASIS?

Our options for activity are extensive when we make the decision to retire. But for some people work was so fulfilling that a return to part-time work is something they desire. All jobs are onerous in some respect: the hours, the time card, the pressure, the paperwork, but underlying these objections, there is a feeling for the work itself which is recalled in retirement.

The experience of this minister of 41 years clearly shows a desire for retirement and a continuing interest to serve in some religious capacity. The availability of "in-service" and "interim minister" work provides a challenge and allows freedom from actual parish administration. His attitude of always retaining some tie to worship and pastoral care is realized with this part-time work. This minimum work load, along with time for family, travel and other interests, provides the balance for his satisfactory retirement.

The retirement advice he offers of acquiring "a sense that when you stop working full time the significance of your life doesn't end" is valid regardless of your attitude toward your former job. If you view retirement as "a kind of a new beginning," you will be encouraged to find those activities which bring purpose and meaning to your life.

19

Thoughts on Aging

When you retire, part of the adjustment process will include some acceptance of the season of life you are entering. This does not imply that your talents, ambitions and dreams are finished. What is called for is a redefinition of your outlook and attitudes toward your own aging.

You may discover for the first time in the presence of older people that you are uncomfortable, dissatisfied with the sight of men and women of your age. Your reaction is understandable, in part, because whatever type of job you held before retirement, you were exposed to people of various ages. Your feelings, however, may reflect an attitude of "ageism—the prejudices and stereotypes that are applied to older people sheerly on the basis of their age" (Butler, 1969).

Another explanation offered about attitudes toward older people is that of "gerontophobia—unreasonable fear and or constant hatred of older people" (Bunzel, 1972). The foundation for attitudes on ageism and to a lesser degree gerontophobia may be based on one's personal history. In my opinion, they are partially explained by a denial of one's own aging.

Attitudes of denial about aging are understandable if one enjoys good health and has the vitality to continue to work or to participate in a variety of leisure activities. In fact, some of us have difficulty realizing we have reached the age of 60, 70, or 80. Our outlook is fresh and alive, and where we may acknowledge some physical decline, we do not feel our chronological age. The truth remains, however, we have joined the group of older citizens.

Dr. Erdman Palmore of Duke University has discussed the issues of the perception of aging: "Many people don't want to admit that they'll ever get older, but actually it's the only thing everybody really does want to do, given the unfortunate alternative. People avoid the subject because they believe all of the depressing stereotypes and myths with which our essentially youth-oriented society has brainwashed us. They equate being old with bad things—poor health, mental incapacity, inactivity, boredom" (Overholser & Randolph, 1979). His suggestions to counter false beliefs about aging include meaningful activities, health maintenance, financial planning and mental attitude—an optimistic outlook.

What is suggested for sound mental health is acceptance of our aging and that of others around us. In truth, most of us look somewhat different than we did 20 years ago—our hair color has changed—our skin tone has altered—our senses of sight and hearing are not as acute—our general energy level is reduced. If you are honest with yourself, you recognize these changes and accept them, on one hand, gratefully, and on the other, as graciously as you can.

III

MARRIAGE

"Women are not used to having men around the house . . . "
"My husband plans, and I try to adjust . . . "
"I'm lucky because of my wife . . . "
" . . . the biggest adjustment I've had involves my husband . . . "
"There was a time we didn't communicate . . . "
" . . . it is important for husband and wife to talk about their interests and goals . . . "

The decision to retire and the related significant meaning of one's work contribute to one's rationale for retirement. As we have seen, retirement decisions are multifaceted: employer mandated, health disability, acceptance of early retirement, the result of poor planning and the desire for relief from the role of worker. Likewise, work-retirement patterns are varied: ambivalence between the involvement of work and unscheduled activities in retirement, the value of part-time work in the transition and an acceptance of retirement as merely being a change in schedules of living.

Now let us proceed to the more personal—marriage and retirement. There is no question that retirement presents a further challenge to marital relationships. Whether partners experience discord or delight depends, of course, on their prior personal harmony. But of equal importance is their determination and ability to communicate individual needs with mutual respect as they share the path of retirement.

20

Marriage and Retirement

A successful marriage is often a miracle and a mystery. When you consider how two people survived the mini and major crises of daily living you might wonder what was their secret. How did they confront the frustration of earning a living? How did they manage their many roles —worker, spouse, parent, citizen, and perhaps presently as parents to their parents? How have they respected and responded to the individual needs of their spouses?

Some clues to marital relationships may be gleaned from the conversations that follow on the retirement of either or both spouses. On the positive side, we witness a couple who had worked together and retired to enjoy the fruits of their labor, appreciative of their companionship; a retired couple who, after solving problems of communication, were thankful for their lot to share the simple life; and finally, a woman who retired after the retirement of her husband because she felt their relationship would suffer if she continued to work.

On the other side of marital adjustment in retirement we are exposed to unresolved conflict: a man who discussed selling his business with his wife, whose principal problem was adjusting to spending free time with her; a retired woman who struggles to maintain her research interests as opposed to ever-present family demands; and finally, a pattern of dissimilar interests of husband and wife and the resultant tensions.

The work-retirement patterns of some of the married women that follow address not only their future plans, but more important, examine the broad spectrum of marital retirement.

RETIREMENT PLANS OF MARRIED WOMEN

If you are married and working, would your husband's decision to retire prompt you to retire at the same time? This question was part of a study I presented to more than 1,200 white-collar working women.

The results indicated a majority of married women, 55%, would not retire based on their husband's decision to retire.

There were two groups involved in this study. The professional group consisted of lawyers, psychologists, certified public accountants, physicians, engineers, college faculty and nurses. The general employment category was composed of employees of a bank, a utility company, a hospital, a chemical company and an automobile manufacturer.

The jobs these women held appeared to play a part in their decision not to retire. The professional group indicated 61% would not retire as compared to 47% by the general employment categories.

Age was a significant factor in the spousal decision to continue to work. Women in both groups, in the age range of 50–59, strongly indicated they did not plan to retire.

Higher income, in the range of $20,000-$25,000, appeared as a significant reason for these married women's decision not to retire.

If a large segment of married women continue to work after the retirement of their husbands, what might be the consequence? Might the roles of husband and wife change? Would the adjustment of the husband to retirement be necessarily made more difficult? One matter is clear: The work role of either partner strongly affects his or her mate when retirement is considered.

If married women continue to work after the retirement of their husbands for reasons of support, they will then function as the principal provider. However, when women continue to work for reasons of personal choice, particularly where the retired husbands have not satisfactorily developed a lifestyle apart from their former work, personal difficulties may result.

Satisfactory answers to the many questions about retirement will, of course, depend on individual circumstances and the relationship during the years of marriage. If husband and wife shared mutual respect and had developed honest lines of communication, decisions about retirement will be approached and handled as they face other turning points in their shared lives.

Retirement is a period of challenge; to the extent the retiree enjoys the support of his or her spouse the transition might well be accomplished more smoothly.

What is called for is an atmosphere of understanding by both partners, recognizing the former patterns of the working husband and the home-maker-working wife have changed. The needs and aspirations of both must be appreciated to realize a meaningful relationship.

21

Spousal Problems in Retirement

Male, age 75, married, one child

Education:	high school graduate
Job Status:	manufacturer for 38 years
Retirement Income:	$100,000
Health:	reported good
Retirement Category:	regular-voluntary, 4 years, returned to part-time work

My business was started from a humble beginning. I worked to make a living and improve myself and become successful so I could enjoy the amenities of life.

My work was very meaningful to me for the first 25 years. After that time, I was disenchanted with the everyday work. It got a little boring for me, and this is when I became involved in outside activities. I think the challenge was gone. I had reached the point in the business where I knew it was not going to be a tremendously large company. I found that I could operate it just as well with less time on my part. The last 15 years I was in business, I only spent half a day in the office, and my success was just as great or greater than in previous years. I could have retired after 25 years if I had wanted to.

I wasn't looking forward to retirement. I wasn't saying, I wish I could retire and do what I want. Retirement to me was just to get out of the general everyday pressures, but I wasn't interested in loafing. I wouldn't call mine a retirement—I sold my business after 30 years.

In a way, I felt that I was partially retired when I started to go in for just half a day.

I wasn't really interested in early retirement. I was concerned whether I would have enough to do if I did retire, and whether I could keep myself involved enough to satisfy me. Before I retired, while I was working only half a day, I had involved myself in many civic affairs. I liked doing this, with the result that I kept giving more time to it. I think it had to do with the fact that I had developed a dislike for my work. It was an era where it was becoming more difficult to cope with the various regulations and the unions, and the business got rougher to operate. I don't mean that I made less money; there were too many things to cope with. I had what I might call a one-man business, with about 25 employees. There seemed to be more pressure all the time.

Some 15 years before I retired, I became very active in raising funds for a charitable organization. This was really my first adventure into outside activities. Up to that time, I was involved strictly in my business. I had no hobbies; I didn't play golf; I didn't care for cards. Actually, I was working all the time.

During the early years of developing my business, I didn't spend too much time with my family, outside of the weekends, because I was traveling all through the state. This pattern changed after my business developed and I found that I didn't have to travel.

I really had no thoughts about retirement, nor did I worry about retiring. I didn't relate that selling my business would mean retirement, although I knew I would be out of active work. I didn't really give much thought to retirement because I felt I had so many outside activities that I would be busy and that I wouldn't have a retirement problem.

The only planning for retirement that I got into was financial, related to the sale of my business. After I sold my business, I had to rearrange my investments with the idea that the money would be used for my retirement and for the benefit of my family. Looking down the line, I figured that I probably would not have any earned income as such, so I became involved in my estate planning. I never gave any thought to planning for leisure time, because I felt that my outside activities would preclude any leisure other than a little traveling.

I didn't give any thought to a second career. At the time I was making the arrangements for the sale of my business, in discussions with my family, my daughter and son-in-law were very concerned that I would be unhappy in retirement. My son-in-law felt that I would not be happy in complete retirement. He felt that work was such a part of my life that just doing this extracurricular work would not be satisfying. This turned out to be true.

I listened to what they had to say. I actually reevaluated my idea of selling out and tried to make sure that I was doing the right thing. I felt that probably what they were saying was true, and that I might not be happy. But the factor of selling my business and getting the dollars that I wanted for my financial security in the later years far exceeded my worries as to whether or not I was going to get along psychologically. I also thought that when I retired I would accelerate the work of my civic activities, which would probably lead to involvement on a full-time basis.

I discussed the idea of retiring with my wife. I believe her feelings were influenced by my presentation as to what it would do for us financially, and that it would not affect our standard of living, and we could still do the things that we wanted. She never prodded me to retire. I don't think that she really cared that much, because I was doing pretty much what I wanted to do.

My original plan was that I would be able to live comfortably off the income. However, it was apparent that the purchasing power of the dollar was decreasing, and it might be that in future years I might have to invade the capital to live in the same manner as before I retired. That time has not yet arrived, although I can see down the line, if I live long enough, I am not going to be able to live off the income. Although I never read anything particularly about retirement, because I was interested in old people and had worked with them in my outside activities, I did have a considerable insight as to what retirement meant. It wasn't a new thing to me.

During the four years before I went back to work on a part-time basis, I found that while I was doing all the things that I wanted to do, they weren't on a regular enough basis to satisfy my needs for daily involvement. I found that the organizations I had leadership roles in kept me busy to some extent, but it wasn't every day, and sometimes two or three days would go by and I didn't have any meetings and I didn't have much to do. I became very bored and unhappy. I believe that the outside work I was doing appeared to have less significance as to its value after I retired than before. I got the feeling that I was doing this work now because I had nothing else to do. I also got the feeling that my civic activities were not as important to me as they were before. This got to be very disturbing.

When I was working in my business I thought that some people might say, "Well, it's great of this guy, he spends so much of his working day for the community and still does his other work." After I retired, I got the feeling that the impression might be, "He's doing this work because he has nothing else to do." It wasn't exactly true, because I know that the people who were working with us, particularly the professionals, were very happy that I had the time to give to them. I had a feeling that I didn't have the stature among my contemporaries that I had before. It is something that is hard to explain, but I didn't feel as good about the work as I did before when I was working in my business.

I tried to analyze the situation. I had plenty of time to think about it. I thought maybe engaging in some hobbies might add to my life. But for a man who belongs to a country club for 20 years and never played golf, or didn't play cards very often—and that's about all these guys do—I just wouldn't do it to occupy my time. It's like someone saying, "Well, now that you are retired, you might take up music." If you were never interested in music before, it isn't very likely you are going to do it now.

My health has always been very good, but I am probably more aware of my health now than I was before. You get more concerned because you have more time to think about it.

The biggest adjustment I had during the four years of retirement was that I felt it was a little difficult to adjust to spending the free time with my wife. Women are not used to having men around the house in the morning, and I am an early riser. I am in the house in the morning. I set up an office at home to take care of my work. I found that either because my wife wanted to keep me involved, or because she wanted to be involved, now she wanted me to do things with her and for her during the day which normally she would not have asked me to do if I was working. I don't think this is unusual. I don't know what the reason for this is. Maybe it's because they want their husbands to be happy, or maybe it's because they want someone to do things for them. While we had no major disagreements about it, I had to sometimes say, "I can't do that today," or "I can't see you because I have things to do." I didn't want to be a chauffeur or an errand boy just because I had the time. My wife would say, "Would you do this?" and I would say, "I can't." She would say, "Well, you have nothing else to do, you can do it for me." This was difficult for me. After all, I had been a boss all my life—not that I was the boss at home. In fact, our relationship was a good one for 48 years. It was a little demeaning to me to be asked to run errands because my wife was going to be playing cards that afternoon, or something like that. I have discussed this with other people, and I think other retired men have the same problem.

During the four years that I was retired, I was involved in big organizations, sometimes taking leadership roles, and attending certain regular meetings that are scheduled at various times during the month.

These are on my calendar. I work by a calendar; I even cross off the days like the guy in jail. I am a very organized person, and so I know in advance whether I have anything to do. If I weren't involved in these activities, or weren't working in my new job, the days would be boring.

The only advice I can give to a man who retires, if he sells his business or leaves his job, is to make sure that he has some place to go in the morning, even if it's only an office where he can sit and read the newspaper. Don't stay at home. I recommend that very strongly.

My wife thought that I was wasting too much time in retirement. She felt that I had too much productive ability and time to let it go the way it was. She was somewhat instrumental in my coming out of retirement and going back to work.

Really, I never got used to retirement. The first year I relished the idea that I was free and did not have to account to any particular schedule, but that wears off after a while. I think the second, third and fourth years were harder times for me. Things got worse as time went on. In a way, I think it is quite a luxury to be able to do anything you want, when you want it, like going out of town for a couple of days, and so I think there are some advantages. But since my background was one where I had always regimented myself and went on a strict schedule, it was difficult for me to be retired.

I had many thoughts about my life when I retired. At times I felt that I was washed up and that my contribution to the business world was ended. You get a feeling that you are not important anymore to the way of life as we know it. It is probably one of the things that every person, unless he stays in his job and works to the end, is bound to realize. You are not as important to life itself. As a matter of fact, you get the feeling that you have had your day and you are washed up. It is now for the younger people.

If I had it all to do over again, selling my business and retiring, I don't think I would have done it any differently. Having retired and knowing many of the drawbacks, and even though I don't like it, I still think I did the right thing.

I really don't have any definite recommendations to others about retirement. It seems to me that anything I might say would be too closely related to my personal situation. I know a lot of men who are retired, and they don't do anything but engage in athletic sports. I feel that a person has to have something constructive to do, related to the field that he was in before he retired. If he were in business, he should have some relationship with business, probably his own business or his own field. However, to be a consultant to a firm where you are not going to do any consulting is merely a sham. My definition of the word consultant is a guy who, when you want to know about something, you ask him, but if you don't ask him, he keeps his mouth shut. You find that they are consulting you less and less all the time.

It's difficult, as a man gets up in years and is still active, to look down the road and wonder what you are going to be doing five years from now. If your health is good—and there is always the concern your health is not going to remain the same—you are thinking about a lot of things you never thought about before.

My adjustment to retirement would have been smoother if I had made arrangements to have a definite place to go so that I didn't have to spend the time at home. I think it would have been a lot easier for my wife and family. It is important for me to retain some degree of daily regularity—to know that I am going to get up in the morning and go to the office. While I may not have a lot of responsibility, the fact that I am expected to be at a place is important.

When I went back to work, it was on a part-time basis, five days a week from about nine until noon. Actually, I didn't seek this job—it was offered to me. A mutual friend suggested that this organization was looking for someone and considered that I would be an asset to them. The job was offered to me, it was very attractive, and I grabbed it. This job was set up on the basis that I could arrange my own timetable. Due to the fact that most of my civic work is in the afternoon, I thought I would reserve this morning time for the business work, and this was satisfactory to this organization. They said to work on my own time, so I come here in the morning and usually stay until noon. I come back sometimes if I have some specific appointment. I generally don't care for weekends altogether; I would rather be working.

I am leaving this job the first of the month. I don't know what I am going to do next. I am not happy because it doesn't give me the involvement that I need. I had hoped that since I was invited to come here that greater use of my knowledge and abilities would be utilized. It hasn't worked out that way. When I leave, I figure I'll be right back where I started a year ago as far as being adjusted to retirement.

WHAT IS THE BASIS FOR SPOUSAL PROBLEMS IN RETIREMENT?

A common family problem of husband-wife relationships upon the retirement of either spouse is unique in that it is a blameless situation.

Neither partner is intentionally responsible for the friction that sometimes results. This vexing situation crosses socioeconomic levels.

This story of retirement illustrates some of the difficulties upon the retirement of the husband. While this man was confronted with the need to reorient his lifestyle from the regularity and responsibility of his business, his adjustment was further compounded by the behavior of his wife.

As he states his case, "women are not used to having men around the house." His analysis overlooked the possibility that his wife was feeling some confusion over his retirement. He could not understand whether his wife merely wanted to keep him involved, or be involved herself by her request that he do things for her and with her. This bewilderment, after a good marital relationship of 48 years, was exacerbated by her statement that he might as well help her since he had nothing else to do. Here was another blow to his ego along with the uncertain status he was experiencing in retirement.

How men and women solve their family problems through the years is an individual matter, but the value of communication is basic to facing the advent of retirement. It is worthwhile to appraise what their past life has been together, as well as to appreciate their individual responsibilities and the varied roles they have played. What activities have they shared which provided mutual meaning and satisfaction? What new directions might they take to seek pursuits which offer purpose and pleasure in their later years?

This approach to a major area of adjustment in retirement provides an opportunity for sharing, interest and concern for each other. It is one of the keys to a rewarding retirement.

22

Married Women and Retirement

Female, 70, married, six children

Education:	college graduate
Job Status:	community college professor for 22 years
Retirement Income:	$17,000
Health:	reported good
Retirement Category:	regular-voluntary, retired for two years

My work was my main interest, but I always had self-doubts. In the teaching racket you always wonder whether you are really teaching them truths, or whether there is something you don't know that you should know. You also wonder whether you are teaching them at the level and at the clarity of expression that you would like.

I enjoyed teaching and the contact with students, but I kept wanting to do research. What with the fifteen hours in the classroom, the five in the office counseling, plus giving essay exams, I was too busy to have the chance to do research.

I had always said I wanted to die in a harness. But I was being balked on this research and so I was looking for a way to do the research before I got too old. And so, in a sense, it was a retirement. As somebody once said, you should not retire *from* something—you should retire *to* something. I retired to do research.

When I was 17 I decided I wanted to be a psychiatrist. I thought I had the ability and could make it, but at the same time I wanted at least four children; I knew that I personally could not combine the two. When I got into medical school, I more or less said goodbye to the family. In the second semester I met and married a man who was willing to have four children. So I became a mother. We had six children. Some years later I went back to school and got my Ph.D.

I didn't worry about retirement. I knew I could not stand it. I would go bananas with nothing to do but sit around and entertain myself.

I had some worries about my health before I retired. I had a serious operation on my right hand and was having back problems to the point where I spent a good bit of my time lying on the floor trying to recover. I did find toward the end I was worrying about whether I would be able to hear sufficiently, to hear what the students were asking me. I have had this hearing problem since I was 23, and it was obviously accelerating in loss. I was trying to find a hearing aid that would handle the matter sufficiently.

My activities other than work consist of spinning and weaving on a backstrap loom, and there are family activities. A rather low level of social life has gone through our whole married life. My husband is not a group person, so there are restrictions on what we do. We have a few close friends with whom we attend the symphony.

I think developing friendships is a problem with all working women. You don't really have time to build friendships. If you have friends at work they are all busy and so are you. You don't have time to see them after work.

What I have seen of retirement was disengagement from active participation and I didn't want that. I have never been good at coffee klatches or bridge playing or any of these time fillers. I get my thrills out of accomplishing something in my work. I have dozens of ideas I would like to be able to work out. If I were not able to work at them, it would be like being in prison.

As far as planning for retirement, we thought about where we were going to live. I had watched my mother and father ride down the highways for years in an Airstream trailer and then settle in a Leisure World in California. Dad died a year later after they moved in. Mother stayed for eight years, enjoying the activities and having a lovely time. When she became unable to maintain it she came back east to us. The break from a leisure community where there were plenty of activities to a place where she knew nobody and there was nothing happening was not a good thing to watch.

Our original plan was that when my husband retired we would move to a small college town where I would get a job in a four-year college and a chance to do my research. This didn't work out because my husband didn't retire, and by the time he did retire there were dozens of Ph.D.'s looking for jobs and nobody was going to hire anybody my age. Furthermore, we have built in, settled in enough in our community. My feeling was you needed to settle in where you wanted to die early enough to make the transition.

My main concern about retirement was whether I could find some place to do my research—or would I be stranded? Would I get absorbed in my desultory home routine and end up going down highways with my retired husband? I loathe driving and my back hurts.

My husband left it up to me about my decision to retire. He said financially we could afford it. I thought our expenses would be less. We were going to go with one car, but still have two. We were going to spend less on clothes, but I've never spent much to begin with.

What we are doing is banking part of our income, investing. I have a firm stand with my husband, who is a much better spender than I am. We have income from multiple sources: his retirement pension, his service pension and Social Security. I've got Social Security and my retirement pension.

My concern about retirement was that I had to keep busy. I had to have a feeling that what I did made some difference somewhere, and that I had to have contacts with people. I could be a recluse if I don't actively work to get out.

If I am retired, I guess it's a good thing, but I am finding the same conflicts I've always had. I am work oriented and my stride is being broken by family demands. My husband wants to travel, and this is not my cup of tea. I have to squeeze my research in between the trips. My husband plans, and I try to adjust.

My advice to others is don't retire. I think you have to have a broad span of perspectives on retirement. You have people who are wanting to get out of what they are doing and just have free time. You have others who are wanting to retire so they can do something else. And some people are forced into retirement. But if you have your choice of when and how to retire, I think it is important to think of what you are retiring to. Have a plan of what you are going to do afterwards. You are not always capable of doing this because it's always at the whim of whether you've got the energy, the health and the money.

I think married women have a problem when it comes to retirement. They know that their housework is there forever. It is a question of whether you are going to have a chance at going beyond the roles that females have forever. The thought of giving up on anything beyond routine housework and nurturance of somebody is a hard one. You can justify it if you've got a job and bringing in needed money. When you stop bringing in money, you can feel yourself being jammed back into that nurturing female who does all that work that nobody else wants to do.

Since I retired I miss the contact with students. I learned what was going on in the world from them. I worry about not being as aware of the world as it is currently without my student informants.

I think some sort of preretirement planning should be available when people start thinking of retirement. It is my feeling that about every 20 years everybody gets restless no matter what they have been doing—a change of pace—a change of focus is needed to keep up morale. Somewhere around 55 you start beginning to think how long am I going to be in this rat race, so retirement looks like a good idea. A program should be available when people are ready for it—like sex education, it should be available on demand.

DOES A MARRIED WOMEN EVER REALLY RETIRE?

When a married woman who has been employed for a number of years retires, does her life change? How free is she to pursue her own interests? Are any of her life roles altered by her retirement?

The underlying question addresses what role changes might reasonably be expected when a working wife retires. Certainly the pressures and structure of the job are over—the demands of the work role are discarded. Parental responsibilities, in a direct sense, are pleasantly cast aside when children have established their own lives. What roles are left to be enjoyed and participated in individually and with one's spouse?

This retiree expressed her feelings on her personal interests, her ambivalence with the retirement experience and some of the conflict involved. As she stated her sentiments: "My main concern about retirement was that I had to keep busy. I had to have a feeling that I made some difference somewhere, and that I had to have contact with people." This desire for people involvement was not in accord with her husband's wishes, "so there are restrictions on what we do." Further, as she strongly stated her position, "it's a question of whether you are going to have a chance at going beyond the roles that females have forever." Is retirement for some married women a time of stress and frustration? How married men and women resolve their differences and desires through the years is a personal and individual affair. However, to the extent that there exists some appreciation by both partners of their individual and mutual needs, a healthy resolution of retirement adjustments may be achieved.

23

Spousal Relationships

Male, 68, married, two children

Education:	college graduate
Job Status:	dry cleaning business, for 30 years
Retirement Income:	$60,000
Health:	reported good
Retirement Category:	early-voluntary, retired for six years

Our work was our main interest because we had to work at it full time to make a living. Up until the last five years it was a big struggle, but we worked hard and our business was successful.

We had never given much thought to retirement. We thought at around 65 we would probably retire, but we had never given it any serious consideration. I didn't worry about it.

My health was a concern. I had known for about 12 years before I retired that I would have to have heart surgery to replace a valve. I knew if something went wrong we'd be in serious trouble. But the years passed and it was close to the age of retirement when I went into the hospital.

Our social activities were limited because of our work; our energy had to be devoted to the business whether we liked it or not. We had a nice group of friends and usually went out on Saturday night. I ran the business for the first 10 years or so. We had two children and my wife was confined at home with them and caring for her mother who lived with us. Once the kids were in high school we worked together full time.

We didn't make any definite preparations for retirement. We were accumulating enough money so that when we did retire we would not have to worry about where our next meal was coming from. We had not worried about hobbies, or what we were going to do.

I thought retirement would be a good idea because the tremendous responsibility would be off my shoulders. The thought of not working did not concern us in any way. We knew that in one way or another we would keep occupied. We knew that we were not going to sit around, watch television all day and twiddle our thumbs. But we had not planned anything specific.

We retired because out of a clear blue sky we had three offers to buy our business. We talked it over; it was a mutual decision. We were sure we could maintain our standards of living.

When we sold the business we went to Florida for two weeks. We had never been able to get away for a winter vacation. We felt we'd feel our way and see what we would do to keep ourselves occupied. As I said, we were not going to vegetate.

It's now been six wonderful years. We love retirement. Time goes by beautifully—we're occupied, and we are always urging others to retire.

When we worked we were on a very regimented schedule. We had to be up early in the morning and we had to be in bed fairly early at night. Now we sleep until seven-thirty or eight o'clock in the morning, but we don't loll in bed all day.

Our main activity is volunteer work with older people. That occupies Monday and Tuesday morning and Wednesday afternoon, and on Thursday morning we deliver Meals on Wheels. The rest of the week we keep open so we can do whatever we please. This volunteer work is gratifying. We see how lucky we are compared to most people.

I don't think we have had any trouble adjusting. There has not been one day where we've felt bored or lost. During the summer we are able to play golf and get outdoors more often. We visit our son and daughter-in-law and grandson in the East two or three times a year. In February we go somewhere to get away from the cold for a month or so.

Retirement hasn't made me feel any older. I am just living another stage of life. We went through the stage of working and finally we are able to benefit from it. Now we have another part of our life to enjoy.

I don't think I would have retired sooner even if I had had the opportunity. I think a person under 60 is not ready for retirement—you've got too much energy and too much going inside of you to retire. It seems to me it takes a certain amount of maturity, a certain attitude before you can really enjoy retirement. Health is the most important thing, and finances.

When you retire it's just a matter of making yourself feel you have some purpose in life, not just being a parasite.

I'm lucky because of my wife. We've been married for almost 44 years, and from the first minute it's been happiness all the time, so working or not working, it doesn't make any difference. I'm very, very happy.

ARE YOU CONCERNED ABOUT MARITAL RELATIONSHIPS IN RETIREMENT?

The oft-repeated expression, "I married you for better or worse, but not for lunch," explains some concerns married women have when their spouse retires. The husband wonders whether he is prepared for 24 hours of togetherness when his wife's main activities are home-centered. This subject of spousal relationships affected by retirement is a source of perceived problems in the future.

What might be the expectation when husband and wife work together and retire together? The conversation of this retiree relates a happy relationship of 44 years. What is apparent is the mutuality of their relationship. They shared the work load, agreed on the decision to sell their business, and have found purpose and pleasure in their retirement activities.

The difference in experience of this retiree was that he did not have to respond to change in his relationship with his wife. If they were to make adjustments and accommodations to a different way of life, without work constraints, they would make them together—this had been their pattern.

The compatibility, or lack of it, of marriage partners is based on their outlook, individual and mutual experiences, and ability to respond to change. Retirement is a period of change—sights, sounds and circumstances. While some retirees express anticipation to more fully share interests and activities with their spouse, they will be confronted with changes in their daily living. Recognition of change and determination to meet the challenge of adjustment will form the basis for a meaningful relationship in the years ahead.

24

Leisure—A Cause for Marital Discord

Female, 65, married, three children

Education: college graduate

Job Status: business operator for 13 years

Retirement Income: $45,000

Health: reported good

Retirement Category: early-voluntary, retired for 15 years

I was drafted by my husband to manage a small business he had invested in. At the time I knew nothing about the product that was being sold, or its use in the construction business. I had had some prior business experience in bookkeeping and office management.

A week after he had made the investment and the papers had been signed, the manager quit. There were only two other employees at that time and they worked in the shop. When he called me, I was preparing the evening meal. He said, "You must get down here right away." There was no choice at that given moment. I expected it to be a two- or four-hour thing, or possibly a couple of days a week. It turned out to be a full-time job.

While I was working, I didn't consider retirement until my parents became ill. Then I realized that life would not continue forever. I think the shock of their deaths really gave me pause to think about my work and what my life was all about.

I resented the confinement of the job; I had no way of having an assistant so that I could have free time. I worked five days a week, maintained my house, and assisted my husband with his paperwork not associated with this business he had purchased. All this limited the time I had to devote to what I was really interested in: my children, study in other directions, and my leisure time.

I never worried about retirement. I felt that I could live on forever. At that point in my life I really didn't see any end to what was current, living from day to day.

My physical health had been good through the years, but not my mental health. I had periods of time when I was depressed and frustrated, and that probably led to my thinking about retiring.

Before I retired, I went back to school and got my master's degree in liberal arts. Our local university had an extended program for working people; I enjoyed the classes and the association with other workers. Before I married, I had worked and gotten a college degree.

My time was limited when I was working. I wasn't able to travel to see two of my children and my parents who lived out of town. I was frustrated by the fact that I couldn't spend time with them.

About two years before I retired, we started to talk about our future life; the amount of time we had left and what life would be like. I wanted early retirement, so we talked about our financial situation and our health. These were all-important considerations. I knew what our net worth was and what our expenses were; we did not have limitless income. We had saved our money though the years so that my husband could retire early. When I brought up the subject of my retiring, after my parents' death, he said he felt the same way, so we made further plans to save toward our retirement.

When I retired I was thrilled and enthusiastic about it. My major concern was for the person I was turning the business over to. He had become a partner; I felt very responsible for leaving the business to him. The arrangement was made for him to pay us out, so that we received income from the business.

I retired three years before my husband. My life became easier when I stopped working because, although I still helped my husband with his paperwork, I had free time to adjust.

When he retired, we traveled for the first year. We visited my family home that I hadn't seen in 25 to 30 years. We visited our children. So the first year was very enjoyable.

I think early retirement is for everyone if you can afford it. It's a wonderful way to spend your growing-up years. My physical health has been good, and my mental health is much improved.

My first problem when I retired was trying to do too much. I over-volunteered myself, but I enjoyed it. I felt I was actually doing something worthwhile. But I slowed down after a while.

Probably the biggest adjustment problem I've had involves my husband. I felt a little guilt at leaving him in order to do the things I wanted to do. He didn't have many outside interests. I had to learn to deal with the fact that those were his problems. I eventually learned that it was my life and I felt I should do the things I was interested in. Right or wrong, that's the way I proceeded.

When my husband worked he became accustomed to the fact that I was home when he was home. When he retired he expected the same pattern; this was the problem. I believe he has not sought out enough outside interests so he hibernates. I don't think that is good for the mind or the soul.

I generally plan my time carefully—what I should do, what I can do—such as the proper amount of exercise, preparing food, and taking care of the house. I try to have free time. I like to work with flowers, read, and do those things that I wasn't able to do when I was overextended in volunteer work. I think I am more relaxed now.

I have tried to encourage my husband to get involved helping others, but up until this time he has not shown any interest. He has expressed some discontent with me for my interest in volunteer work. I believe there is a great need in our country for volunteers. There is a world of different fields that one can get into.

When I went back to college I didn't anticipate going into business. I hoped to become a psychologist and develop a career in that direction.

I think it is difficult for young people to plan for retirement. When I recall my own feelings, I thought time would take care of everything; there would be no problems. In today's world young people see such a turnaround in national politics, in the national and international business scene, that I think they have a terrible time thinking about the future. When I talk to people in their 50s today, it's hard for them to even consider retirement. I am amazed that they are able to project their lives into the future.

The best advice I could give anyone about planning for retirement is to start a savings program as early as possible, even if it is a small amount per month. I know it is very difficult today.

DO YOU HAVE A PROBLEM WITH 24 HOURS OF TOGETHERNESS?

One subject overlooked by some working couples when they consider retirement is what they will do with their time. Where both partners enjoyed some success and satisfaction during their years of work, of family nurturing and leisure, retirement may be an event which produces confusion and personal discomfort. In fact, difficulty of spending so much time together is expressed by some men and women before they retire.

It is perhaps difficult for the husband and wife to realize what changes might occur in their relationship what with this newfound unlimited time together. In a general way they may have retired to seek relief from working, plan on travel, and look forward to the absence of their former routine. But to what extent will retirement offer some fulfillment of their individual expectations, needs and interests? Will their paths of leisure activities coincide or cross and be a source of conflict?

The conversation of this retiree reveals that while there was mutual agreement about early retirement, and communication about financial matters, no understanding or harmony existed about their leisure time. We witness a double problem: a husband who "hibernates" has few outside interests and expects his wife to be at home, and a wife who values volunteer activity and her decision to pursue this interest.

Since most marriages survive on some degree of accommodation, the advent of retirement may be viewed as but another turning point in the relationship. Some recognition is required to accept this period as one of challenge, requiring understanding of our individual needs and respect for those of our partner.

25

Spousal Communication in Retirement

Female, 63, married, three children

Education:	high school graduate
Job Status:	school secretary for 15 years
Retirement Income:	$8,000
Health:	reported good
Retirement Category:	early-voluntary, retired for 12 years

My work filled an emptiness that I had. I wasn't happy just staying home. I'm the kind of person who likes to be involved in office-type work and it filled my days. I enjoyed my work in school working with teenagers.

I was looking forward to retirement. My job at the time involved a conflict of personalities. I knew that when my husband retired he would be home alone all the time, so I decided at the end of the school year to get out.

We never worried about retirement because we had planned ahead of time for it.

My health had been a problem before I retired. I had high blood pressure and I noticed other symptoms which were making the job stressful. I asked to have some of my work changed, but I was told if I didn't like my work I should get out.

My biggest thrill since retiring is not having to get up early and pack lunches. It doesn't take much to please me. When we bought our mobile home up north, that was a great joy.

We always planned ahead. We worked out finances from day one; we have always kept a budget. We knew that if something happened to either one of us there would be no problem.

I was anxious for my husband to retire. He was tired, he was ready. I could have worked on—my job wasn't that much of a strain.

Finances were our biggest concern. Could we do it? We knew we would be cut back to a once-a-month pay instead of every week. We wanted to keep our pledges to the church. We never had a high lifestyle, but we knew we would be satisfied. Our life consisted of playing cards with the neighbors or going to a show. Our pensions covered our medical insurance and that was important. My husband took out a special widow's pension, which meant that if something happened to him I would still get a pension and I would be able to get along.

When we retired we just wanted to sit back and enjoy. Our mobile home worked out well until my husband had a stroke a few years later. I noticed that things were twice as hard for him to do, and I could not help him as I had done before. It was a mutual decision to sell this home.

We have been retired now for twelve years and I've enjoyed it. I enjoy the company of my husband. If I were alone, if something happened to him, it wouldn't be the same.

As far as getting along is concerned, one thing stands out in my mind. My husband wanted to help me do jobs that I had been doing for 30 years. He wanted to help me make the bed. He insisted on getting on one side of the bed, with me on the other, and getting the job done as quickly as possible. I like things straight and he would say, "What's the difference?" I told him, "I've been making beds all these years and you are not going to tell me what to do now." There were little things, but he soon learned that certain things are my territory and it all began to work out—nothing dramatic, no fights.

There was a time we didn't communicate and we were not aware of it; it was causing a strain. You must have an open line of communication after you retire. Little things that normally wouldn't bother you seem enormous when you are together 24 hours a day. There seems to be friction and it grows if you don't talk about it. It took our oldest daughter to see the problem. She said to me one day, "Mom, what's the matter with you and Dad? Aren't you talking anymore?" Finally we decided that was the problem; things are better now.

Now we talk about everything, including death. We have all the details figured out ahead of time to help our girls. I come from a much bigger family than my husband and I know what chaos sets in and we would like to save our children from these problems.

More or less we let life come to us and take it day by day. One of our daughters works for an airline so we travel to see our children and visit my sister.

As far as any advice to others about the future, I think if you want something you should save for it. You don't want to get into debt where you have monthly payments. I think you should buy according to your income; if it's something big, wait until you can afford it. Don't stick your neck out.

WILL COMMUNICATION BE A PROBLEM WHEN YOU RETIRE?

One difficulty expressed by some men and women when they think of retirement is getting along with their spouse. The realization is clear that neither partner will feel the former press of time. Their responsibilities of employment, parenting, and extensive household chores will be over. Now, what with the abundance of time, will communication become a problem?

Do you remember what you talked about when you were working—the job—money matters—the kids—some social plans—decisions on vacations—perhaps your aging parents? The pace was fast, never sufficient time to settle anything. Now in retirement, with options of your choice, with altered roles of responsibility, the setting is so different with the children establishing their own lives, have you considered how these changes might affect your marriage?

Dr. Lillian B. Rubin, a research associate at the Institute for the Study of Social Change at the University of California, discusses spousal interaction related to the empty nest (when children leave home), but the issues are equally valid when applied to retirement. She states: "Some women talk of fears for the marriage. It has been so long since there were just the two of them, will they know how to relate to each other without the children mediating?" She further expressed this anxiety about communication related to her: "Will they be able to talk? I don't know what we'll talk about, just the two of us, after all these years" (Rubin, 1980).

The issues of communication with the retirement of both husband and wife are brought to the surface by the conversation of this retiree. Although she recognized the lifestyle changes in her home by 24 hours a day of togetherness, the cause of conflict as shown by the lack of communication was not apparent. It required the intervention of their daughter to recognize her parents were not talking as they had when both were working. When the underlying fact of failure to talk, to communicate, was brought to the surface, progress in their adjustment was achieved to the point where everything is discussed, including such events as dying and death.

Retirement at its best is a first-time opportunity for choices, for a less stressful existence, and a time for the beauty of honest communication. To the extent we appreciate it, this is one of the rewards of retirement: Our future years are enriched.

26

Spousal Retirement

Female, 62, married

Education: college graduate
Job Status: journalist, for 30 years
Retirement Income: $45,000
Health: reported good
Retirement Category: early-voluntary, retired for one year

My work was my main interest; I enjoyed it and got a great deal of satisfaction out of my job. My husband, before he really knew what I did, used to think that my job was a piece of fluff, just a piece of cake. He found out that it was a difficult and trying job and it took a great deal of tact, patience and understanding. It required a great deal of time to gain the respect of the people with whom I worked when I covered their events. It took years to develop their trust and confidence.

My job was to cover the social events in the city. There were openings at the art museum, the symphony orchestra, and many charity events. When kings and queens and heads of state came to town I was always there to cover parties, do interviews. I've interviewed and spent time with presidents' wives on the campaign tour.

My idea of retirement was that I would retire when I became 65. I had no intention of leaving when I was 60. My decision was based on a number of things.

My paper was sold to a large chain and the feeling of family left the organization. I did not feel that same sense of loyalty and love and affection. My paper had been my family for a lot of years. My sister and brother live in the West, one brother lives in the East, and one in the upper part of the state, so I was literally in the city without any family other than my husband.

When my husband had serious surgery we came to the conclusion that this would be a good time for him to retire. He did not need any more stress in his newspaper job. Newspapering is one of the most stressful jobs. It is stressful due to the fact you have deadlines, and you never know what you are doing any one day. You are on the cutting edge all the time, you are running in high gear. We decided that it would be best if he took an early retirement and the new chain offered him a very attractive buyout. Since he was 65½ at the time and within six months of retirement, it meant no great sacrifice to his pension.

I thought I would work a couple more years until I was 62 and then get my Social Security and pension. I was 60 at the time, so I had a year and nine months before I would be 62. We discussed it at home and realized that my going to the office was not a 9-to-5 thing. I would be out many evenings and my husband would be home alone. We finally concluded that our relationship would suffer if I continued to work. I think we have one of the best marriages alive because we work at it and share many interests in common.

We looked at our finances and at what I would stand to lose or gain by staying there until I was 62. I asked my boss, "What would happen if I retired early?" He said, "I think we could put a very attractive package together for you because you have been a long, valued, loyal employee, someone we treasure around here." So I wrote a letter of resignation and turned it in nine months before I left.

They kept saying, "We don't want you to go, what can we do to keep you here?" But the bottom line was that I felt our marriage would have too many stresses and strains if I stayed on. We married late in life; we are both happy. We thought retirement was the best thing for both of us.

I never considered early retirement in the past. I loved to wake up every day of my life excited about going to work, mainly because of the kind of product I turned out each day. I had the best of all possible worlds—I met interesting people and got satisfaction of seeing my story in print a few hours after I wrote it. It's not like another job where you might see the end product months down the road. I like to write, but it is a lonely business. For me it was worth it to cut myself off from friends and doing things with them on Sunday.

My other activities, when I could find time for them, consisted of some volunteer work with my church and being active in our local professional journalism fraternity and the press club. I have had strong feelings about women in communication and feminism. I support most feminist causes because of my job in the newspaper business. I was never paid what I should have been paid. When I started I received $75 a week, while the men were getting as much as $130.

I thought when I retired I would find time a burden, but this has not been the case. My husband and I are busier today, or as busy as when we had careers. We are on the boards of a number of organizations and work hard for charitable causes in the city. When my husband is involved in a project, I support him, just as he contributes his time to my interests.

As far as planning in general, I am a very well-organized person. My husband says I run the house like an army mess sergeant. I plan things; I write lists. I write menu plans for the week, just as I did when I worked. I don't know how any career woman can work otherwise than to sit down and do some planning in her household. If there is one thing that I might change in my life it would be to take more time about planning for retirement. I was so happy in what I was doing that I just went along thinking retirement would take care of itself. I did not do any planning. I did not know what to expect when we talked about our retirement. We did chat with a number of financial planners about six months before we retired. Our legal affairs were up to date; we both made wills five years ago.

One important thing we did when we retired was move from our townhouse to a condo farther out in the country. I do not like to dwell in cement and steel. There were too many office buildings and large apartment complexes where we had lived. I like gardening and flowers, and I wanted to have more of a pastoral, peaceful scene.

As far as our future activities, we plan to do a fair amount of traveling. On a daily basis we walk for an hour every morning and this should help us maintain our health.

As far as any financial planning is concerned, about the time of our retirement we talked to people in the trust department of a bank and someone at a brokerage firm. We discovered that we had our heads in the clouds and were not practical. We could not even tell them how much money we had. We began at that time to itemize our expenditures and look at what we had in the way of investments. The day I retired I could not believe I was leaving the paper. It was something I had done all my life. I started working after school and Saturdays at a weekly newspaper when I was 15 years old. I have only had two jobs, one on a weekly and the other on this paper.

My major concern at that time was, could I live without writing every day? This may sound strange, but I wondered what am I going to do with my days? I have gotten up, sat in front of a typewriter or a computer all my life; or I have been on the phone interviewing, calling people and arranging to meet them, and going out with photographers, writing photo orders.

I soon found out that I don't have enough hours in the day to do what I want. I am interested in taking some classes in art and music appreciation and hope to gain a better understanding of them. Another area I was a little concerned about when we retired was are we going to have enough money, not for 1989, or 1991, but what about 1995 and 1998? The amount of money we have today is substantial, but how is it going to shrivel down the pike with inflation? We have been shocked at the price of groceries and how they have gone up in one year.

As a working woman I went to the grocery store and I didn't know if the price of tuna fish was 59 cents or $2.59; I bought it. My husband had the same problem. I would ask him, "How much did you spend, Hon?" He would reply, "I don't know, I just paid for the groceries." When ears of corn that I purchased last year for one dollar for a dozen and a half went to four for a dollar, I suddenly became more cost-conscious.

Now that we have actually stopped working, I feel very good about retirement. I feel that we are blessed with good health and believe there are many challenges out in the world. I have found one or two writing assignments that are meaningful to me and I'm itching to get going.

One minor adjustment I had to make was making lunch for my husband. My quick lunches in the past might have found me eating a bowl of cereal standing at the kitchen sink. I suddenly realized my life is more structured because my husband expects a sandwich along about noon. I discovered you have to make plans to stop whatever you are doing and make lunch.

I have some definite thoughts about retirement. I think everyone should have specific information about his or her finances. They should consider getting into some activity right away. In my case, I got into some volunteer work for a local music group. This activity gave me a point of view, something to think about, something I had to plan. I made phone calls, put a committee together, did some writing and held press conferences. If you don't get into some activity, I think you are going to feel lost and begin to wonder, "What am I supposed to be doing today?"

I am a structured person and used to a certain amount of regimentation. My pattern of life consisted of getting up, going to work and meeting deadlines. I think it is important to have some structure in your life; you can't just bounce along.

It is my opinion that when you consider planning for retirement you must be open and honest with your spouse about your feelings. My husband and I didn't hold anything back from each other. We shared how we felt about leaving our jobs. I told him of my fears. I think you have to thrash out all the doubts and try to answer the questions that concern both of you.

I also think it is a good idea to look at your life in terms of goals. Have you reached your goals in your worklife? I was blessed with a job that I wanted to do and never wanted to do anything else. I could have had boss jobs where you sat behind a desk and pulled the strings of somebody else's life. I never wanted that sort of work. My ambition was to be left alone to write, to cover my beat. If you feel that you have reached your goals I think you are ready to step out of your job into retirement.

I think it is equally important for husband and wife to talk about the interests and goals they might share in their retirement years. One thing we both wanted was to change our living arrangements by moving farther out of the city to the country. We are both pleased with this change.

I encouraged my husband to do some teaching in the field of journalism because I felt he needed that dimension in his life. We felt we had something more to contribute. We want to be productive and useful people, and perhaps give a little something to the profession we both loved so much.

WHAT ARE THE CONSIDERATIONS OF SPOUSAL RETIREMENT?

The retirement of one spouse, in a family where both are employed, poses one set of questions. Will the retired spouse alone be able to satisfactorily occupy his or her time after the structure and demands of years of work? After the initial burst of enthusiasm at not having to get up early every morning and go to work, will the retiree become bored, lethargic and overwhelmed by this newfound freedom? Finally, who is to share this leisure period and who is available for support in the transition to retirement?

These are valid considerations. The retirement of both spouses in the same general time frame brings forth other issues of an individual and family nature. The matter of personal concerns, the rationale of the retirement decision, the mutuality of interests and outlook regarding their future lives are well defined in this interview.

The fact that both had been employed in the newspaper business for many years gave them some perspective as to the activities they were leaving. This, however, was a source of concern for the wife. Would time be a burden? Could I live without writing every day? The bases for their mutual decision to retire were clear: the husband's health, the stressful nature of his job, and their belief that their relationship would suffer if the wife continued to work.

Although the absence of any specific planning for retirement was evident, including basic awareness of their financial resources, their desire to communicate honestly about their feelings and goals provided an optimism about the future. Their shared interests to travel, to participate in local causes, to be productive and to contribute to society suggests a satisfying recipe for retirement.

IV

RETIREMENT PLANNING

"I consider myself a planner . . . "
"I didn't plan for my retirement far enough in advance . . . "
"We didn't do any planning for retirement . . . "
"What we did was look ahead . . . "
"I've always tried to make plans ahead of time . . . "
"Retirement—that was the plan . . . "

If you are married, the advent of retirement presents another crisis—a turning point in your life and that of your spouse. Retirement is more than a cessation of employment regardless of the satisfaction and stress the job provided. It is the most personal time for both partners to consider the meaning of their future years together.

Recognition that the years ahead are relatively brief compared to the past, that such matters as health, abundance of leisure time, fewer tasks and less responsibility are now some of the issues of focus facing married couples.

Problems of a major or minor nature do arise in this period, as we have seen: boredom with one's spouse; the struggle to maintain individual interests; dissimilar leisure interests. But, in truth, your life has been a pattern of problems requiring solutions and accommodations, regardless of your marital compatibility. What is now called for is a determined effort to communicate by husband and wife to understand new issues: altered finances, the death of a spouse, future living arrangements, and individual and shared schedules as they seek enjoyable, meaningful use of their leisure time.

The conversations that follow illustrate how some retirees addressed their future years by retirement planning.

27

Planning for Retirement

Today, retirement planning has many titles: "Think of Your Future" (an AARP publication), "PREP for Your Future" (Action for Older Persons, Inc.), a joint U.A.W.—G.M. project titled "Design Your Successful Tomorrow," "Creating Your Future Now" and "Life Planning Program" (Ford Motor Company).

These approaches are similar in content and their focus is on the future. They discuss many of the important issues of living when you retire: financial and living arrangements, leisure, legal and health matters, relationships and adjustments.

The truth of the matter is that many of these significant subjects have been part of your approach to living while you worked. What is called for is a forward look, some redirection and refinement of your thinking for the years ahead. When you retire more attention may be devoted to certain areas—leisure activities and relationships with others.

The benefits of preparation for retirement are overlooked by many. The oversight while one is still employed to think through the possibilities and possible problems is often based on some resistance to the idea of retirement, and a lack of confidence in the ability to plan. This is not to say that detailed preparation is a requisite for everyone. But some awareness of those changes that occur after leaving one's job might well contribute to a person's attitude toward retirement.

The conversations that follow reveal attitudes toward planning and the consequences of this effort. A college instructor covers all bases, including thoughts for living in the later years. His statement, "I see the need to think through carefully what activities mean," was not only his practice before total retirement, but displays a desire to increase and share interests with his wife.

The statement of an appliance salesman, "I didn't spend as much time thinking about retirement as I should have," illustrates financial miscalculation. He realized he lacked skill in financial matters, yet he declined to join retirement groups or pay particular attention to the guidance books furnished by his employers. One writer addressed this latter point: "Corporations have spent thousands in attempting to communicate their retirement programs. Unfortunately, too many times this has fallen on deaf ears or at least had limited retention" (Tatzmann, 1972). However, in fairness to this retiree who sought further company assistance, the following remarks are appropriate: "Effective communication with employees requires a good share of management thought and time, and not of a delegated 'communicator' hired because he or she can write acceptable filler material for a company newspaper" (Darrow, 1975).

Other reflections on the planning factor include a retired bus driver, who indicated no particular planning for retirement, yet benefited by his father's experience: "I've stayed ahead of inflation by making some good investments." A businesswoman's life required no implementation for the future years in view of her attitude, "I think a person should plan their whole life." The philosophy of a retired doctor, "I've always tried to make plans ahead of time," provides some insight for his satisfaction with living. Finally, as an office manager acknowledges, "Retirement was the plan," and it was on this basis that she and her husband proceeded to investigate their plans to relocate.

28

Planning for the Final Years

Male, 62, married, two children

Education:	college graduate
Job Status:	college instructor, 27 years in education
Retirement Income:	$30,000
Health:	reported good
Retirement Category:	early-voluntary, presently on a three-year phased retirement program

It seems to me my job was my main interest. The whole field of gerontology was something I had always been interested in, and when I compare that with other interests that I have, the job was my main concern. I invested most of my energies in it. There was often very little time for family. I was frequently out on the road teaching, lecturing. I did manage on weekends to find some time with my family. The job took what I had off the top, by way of energy and interest, and these other things, although I liked them very much, I just never had enough time really to follow these other interests.

My work was satisfying, and I felt successful because of the signals I got from my peers and students, and the recognition was certainly forthcoming in the general area of social gerontology. I am interested in people. I am concerned about old people, so that my work had a kind of intrinsic meaning to me. However, I perceive my life as having several dimensions. The work dimension has certainly been paramount. I am doing what I like, I get satisfaction from it, and others have indicated that I am doing a creditable job. But in addition to this, I have other consuming kinds of interests. Although my work has taken most of my time and energy, I have been able to design gardens for my friends. I have built many stone walls.

There are some people whom I know who don't have these multi-dimensions. I can think of a number of people who only want to work, who only get satisfaction from working, doing the job, and when they are forced by some circumstance to socialize, they are uneasy. They are uncomfortable, and they don't enjoy other kinds of activities. Now the lesson this teaches me is that we do ourselves a disservice when we invest everything in a job. It may be that this is sort of a folk myth that we are a work-oriented society.

When I was able for the first time in my adult working life to have four months unencumbered, I spent the time engaging in many of my interests; with my family, gardening, hiking, listening to music. And for the first time I had freedom just to sit and think—this was exceedingly precious.

My feelings had not changed in my attitude toward my job three or four years before this phased retirement—such as becoming discontented, having doubts about my abilities or any of the other things that might have changed my attitude toward my job. To the contrary, these were among the very busiest years of my working life. I was spending many, many hours each day of the week in connection with the job. I think that the temporal demands at that time gave me pause to think about whether I was doing a good job because I was getting very tired at times. There was tremendous pressure. My wife had commented on my busy schedule: "You had better slow down . . . you shouldn't be going so fast . . . you ought to find time to do some of the other things you like so well." I never worried about retiring in the sense that it was hanging over my head, that it was inevitable, or that I found the idea distasteful.

I hadn't given phased retirement much thought until this option became available here at the university. I had presumed that I would work full time until age 65. My wife and I had talked about this very carefully. She's a professional person and will retire at the end of this school year.

At the present time, faculty can retire from the university at 55 years of age if they have had 30 years of service. It's not, however, until they become 62 that they can elect to take their retirement furlough pay. The age 62 was selected because at that time an individual is also eligible for Social Security. In other words, at age 62 an individual can take phased retirement and during this period receive Social Security as well as a prorated amount of his retirement furlough pay. In my case, I worked out a plan that had to be approved by my department head. It works out that I have agreed to stay on the job for eight months of the year for the next three years. In other words, I am off for four months and working for eight months a year.

As far as my general activities before I went on this phased retirement, among other things I was involved in church activities. We also had a group of close friends who socialize together from time to time. My wife and I put great store on family activities, especially at holiday time, and we have encouraged our family to be with us, or we go with them as often as we can. I manage to find some time to garden, design gardens for friends and others. I am very much interested in Japanese gardening. I like to take pictures. I enjoy developing portfolios of special kinds of subjects, and I am very much interested in diminutive wild flowers and have collections of pictures of this kind. I have a fine record collection, and when I have time I enjoy playing the piano. When I was working full time I was not able to enjoy the company of our friends or our family as much as I would have preferred.

I was aware of the fact that I wanted to spend more time with my family and have more time to work in the garden when I retired. I recognize, being in the field that I am, that as you become aged, you have to adjust and adapt. There are many activities that I do now in my spare time that I won't be able to do when I get older, so I have been trying to pick up and encourage some other interests. I am learning how to weave. My wife is joining me in this activity. She is learning how to dye with natural materials, wools, and spin them. We will do many things together of this sort. I am very conscious of the fact that some of the things I want to do in retirement ought to be things that I do with my spouse, and of course we are both equally interested in our family and we both love to read. One of the very nice aspects of this phased retirement is that you can explore a new division of your time, for different kinds of activities.

I am interested, not only in connection with my professional work in social gerontology, but as person, I firmly believe that the later years ought to be ones that are in large part contemplative. This is the time when we have lived long enough, and can sort out different aspects of life. I believe that the most important thing is my relationship with people; material things are not so important. During my younger adult years, having a home, having a garden were important to work for. Giving my children an education, clothing them, having a nice car, all these things had a driving and impelling kind of effect on wanting to work and earn. I am a long way from having completed this process. I think, as I get older and older, if my mind continues to function, I will become more concerned with contemplation. However, in order to do this I will have to do a lot more reading.

I see retirement as more freedom, more time in which to elect other options. This for me is sort of the ground on which to build, on which I have built an understanding of retirement. I perceive retirement as a time of opportunity, as more freedom in the ways in which I elect to use my time—freedom from the drives and demands that are made on a professional person in his adult years.

I consider myself a planner, and as far as retirement is concerned, I can support this by the fact that we monitor our expenses carefully. I think we know what we are going to have to live on in retirement. I purposely elected some new activities and am learning them so I will have a wider spectrum of possibilities in my later years, especially when I become more aged and can't do the things I do now which require a great deal of physical effort. Because of the nature of my work, I think much of this activity has rubbed off on me.

One important area that we have thought about is where we are going to live in the future. We are trying to build some options. We have this retirement home up north, and we are perfectly aware that the time will come when we won't be able to live away up on those high hills overlooking the lake, hundreds of feet from the road, with big snow drifts. We are trying to think through our future phases in this connection, and during the first five to ten years, we are asking ourselves, what is feasible, what is manageable, and what assumptions might we make about health and income.

We are trying to think through the age from 65 to 75—what changes will we have to encounter in that period, and from 75 to 85, and then 85 and older. My wife recognizes that during this period she may live alone. We are perfectly aware of the fact that she is likely to outlive me. We are talking about that eventuality, and about what her preference would be if and when I am not around. I think it is useful to engage in this consideration ahead of time. Thinking about these matters ahead of time eliminates the survivor's being caught off guard. When husband and wife follow this approach, they have the security of knowing what their spouse would have wanted them to do, so in our case, where we live is a very important consideration. We have not finalized our plans yet, but we are doing a great deal of thinking about it, and at this stage we are approaching it in terms of blocks of time.

On another matter, I recently brought our legal affairs up to date. I had a will that was compiled when I went in the service. I was married at the time. Through the years I didn't do anything about changing it, but in the meantime we had acquired some property, and so there was every reason to develop a proper will. Three years ago we went to an attorney in town, in whom we had great confidence, and had two wills made, one for myself and one for my wife. We have arranged our property through an estate-planning process which is fairly complicated. We now feel confident that everything is up to par. We have planned things as to how we are going to take care of the surviving spouse, the children and grandchild.

As a result of having to bring our wills up to date, I had to very carefully evaluate my net worth. We had a good idea of our general living expenses because we had systematically kept a record of everything we had spent. We followed this procedure for a number of years, and are back again doing it now. We are involved in record keeping because obviously over the years the cost of living has changed, and our habits have changed our expenditures. We feel we need to know rather accurately when I retire fully at 65 what our expenditures might be. Taxes have gone up, car insurance has gone up, so that the old records aren't useful. We are in the process of developing a new set, and we feel that we need to do this over a period of two to three years.

When this early retirement offer became available, I thought I had the best of everything. I had my job; I could continue to perform for eight months of the year. I had no loss of income whatever during this period, and in addition, I had four months of free time. I didn't see how I could find any better combination during the phased aspect of my retirement. Now, obviously, when I retire fully, the picture is going to change. If at that time I still want to do some things in connection with my work, I think I will have an opportunity to do consulting jobs. I have been offered teaching jobs in other parts of the state. Even now people have heard about my planning to retire, and have asked me if I wanted to teach at their institutions. I suppose that I could find teaching opportunities elsewhere, so that I am anticipating during the first phase of full retirement that I will probably maintain some activities that are job oriented, but I will select what I want to do, when I want to do it. It is this freedom that is so appealing, and I strongly suspect that my life will still be a mix of gerontological activities with my other interests.

I have had the experience now of four months' retirement, and I am perfectly aware of the fact that these four months are probably not typical. The mix of activities and things I do once I become fully retired will probably be somewhat different.

I would not have requested early retirement if it hadn't been offered in the way it was. Indeed, you see, I had no loss of income, and income right now is important in our planning. We are helping our children establish homes, we are finalizing our own building, so if I hadn't had this option with full income, I probably would not have elected it. The main concern I had about this early retirement before I made the final decision was about the money aspect. I had these things I still wanted to do with money. I was concerned about working out with my wife a plan that would reflect the fact that she was considering retirement as well. I was concerned with initiating a careful kind of record of expenditures, so that when the time came we had a better record on which to plan what our expenses were going to be in retirement. I felt fairly confident that we had handled the legal aspects of our household property.

I pondered this early retirement decision for at least three or four months before I announced to the chairman that this is what I wanted to do. I selected the summer months for my time off because there are so many other things that I can do in the summer.

When I discussed the matter with my wife, her principal concerns were about my being so tired the last three years, and how demanding I found the job. I think when my wife and I retire fully, our retired income will be about two-thirds of our working income. I am in the fortunate position of having a fairly substantial army pension, plus a university insurance pension that I contributed to, and we will, of course, benefit from Social Security. My wife also has a teacher's pension, so that our combined income puts us in an advantaged position. When we retire we will have to scale down, and we are already talking about those ways when we do retire to reduce expenditures. For instance, we have two cars now; in the future we will have only one. We will probably spend less for home improvements and gardening and things of that kind. In general, we are planning to live on our income.

After I made the decision, I certainly didn't have any second thoughts or misgivings. It seemed to me then and now to be the reasonable thing to do. I had one reaction, however, which may be of interest. Before I took the phased retirement I was exceedingly busy and involved in many things. Some of the time I was pretty tired, and my style of life was such that when I moved into phased retirement I think I tended to go just as fast but do other things. I have a great deal of drive, whether I am building rock walls or in retirement education program. But after four months were over, it took me some time to get back into the swing of things. I was conscious of the fact that I had to make the effort to get going again. When I came back it just didn't seem the gauge was reading at the same poundage of steam or energy being put out on the job as before. I had trouble in the first part of my return in pushing myself in the evening to get to work again, and I suppose I haven't really achieved the same level of performance outside the job as I did before.

As far as retirement activities are concerned, I think each person has to make his own decision, and there is no one of us intelligent enough to recommend how someone else should retire, or what he should do in the retirement years. On the other hand, from my own experience I see the need to think through carefully what activities mean. To me the meaning of the activity is much more important than the activity itself. The meaning can be defined in terms of whether or not the retirement activity will bring some of the same satisfactions that one's work activity gave during the adult years. I would recommend that any individual who is contemplating retirement ought carefully to consider meaning—what the activity means, what kinds of satisfactions are going to be derived from it. Simply to schedule many activities to fill time is tragic, and can only have tragic results. There are some people who know they have so many waking hours a day in retirement, and they proceed to fill these hours with one thing after another. This doesn't mean that I don't see some value in a schedule, or having committed oneself to do certain things at certain times during the day. I think we are creatures of the clock one way and another, and we can't escape it once we retire. I feel that many of the things we elect to do ought to be carefully determined and defined in terms of their meaning.

Although I have had only these four months of experience, I don't recall a problem with wondering what to do with my time, or in my relationship with my wife and family. This family problem occurs in retirement because it brings people together for the first time over a long period of time every day. I am alert to where these problems can arise.

It is only when I was incapacitated for two or three weeks with a back injury that I became acutely aware of the fact that one's health is a very important dimension. I had known this from an academic standpoint, but it was the first time that I really had any personal experience with illness or fear as a result of a disabling physical condition.

The aspect which has been most pleasurable to me is having the freedom to choose what I am going to do during the day, and not having unreasonable pressures. I have always been an early riser—I would get up at 5:30 or 6:00 in the morning, and I continued to have a schedule during the day even though it wasn't involved with my regular vocation.

Some of the joys of retirement that I have experienced so far include the freedom to select the kinds of things I want to do with my time, the opportunity to spend more time with my family, and to work in the garden. Really, I can't recall any aspects of those four months that gave me any real concern or worry. I guess maybe there were times, if I am perfectly frank, where I wondered if I was being faithful to my career. I would ask myself, should I be keeping up with the literature, be doing more reading? Shouldn't I be finding the time to maintain numerous kinds of things that I ought to be doing in my field? I was perfectly aware of the fact that I hadn't weaned myself completely from my work, and that I didn't intend to. For the next three years I am going to be busy, and have been given some very substantial kinds of responsibility.

I don't think I would have been interested in this early retirement option at age 55, although I had looked forward to retiring. I would have felt that I wanted to stay with the field longer, but I am disposed generally to favor early retirement as an option for those who want to elect it. I think it is important that we have many options to reflect differences in people. I think in our modern industrial society that it isn't necessary for all of us to work until we drop in our tracks. There can be time in our older years, if we want it, and can elect not to work. The trends reflect the fact that no longer does our society need everyone on the labor force throughout their lifetime.

ARE THE LATER YEARS OF LIFE PART OF RETIREMENT PLANNING?

The components of preretirement planning are all interrelated to future living. The relationship of financial income, state of health, use of time, living arrangements, and interpersonal adjustments usually are understood when one is working. There is often little appreciation or awareness of those changes that will take place within the process of retirement. The recognition of the aging factor, the finality of life, is overlooked or avoided when retirement plans are considered. The conversation of this retiree faces those issues of living and dying, and addresses some reasonable expectations of both marriage partners.

This couple has discussed the various options for the years ahead within the framework of present and future living arrangements. They have talked of where they might live, what activities they might manage. These considerations take into account changes which will occur along the way.

Their approach to retirement living focuses their planning on blocks of future time, along with recognition of their ages in each period, after establishing time blocks involving ages 65–75, 75–85, and older. They have tried to take into account where they might be living, what their activities might be, with full allowance for the fact of aging.

The recognition by both that the wife may well be living alone has a direct effect on their proposed living arrangements in the later years. Since this possibility exists, their plans include the wife's preferences for the future so that she is not caught "off guard." This man's appraisal of the situation and discussions with his wife are directed toward some removal of doubt and anxiety about the future.

This planning is founded on the recognition of various options available when they retire. Their method is to think and talk about these choices while both are still working. The question is not how closely they adhere to their block-of-time approach, but rather, with some clarity of choice, how they approach the future years of expected change and have made provisions for them.

Financial Problems and Retirement Planning

Male, 64, married, two children

Education:	high school graduate
Job Status:	appliance salesman, 31 years with an international department store chain
Retirement Income:	$14,000
Health:	reported good
Retirement Category:	early-voluntary, retired for 3 years

My work wasn't exciting. It was a means to an end, but considering the work I was doing, I felt satisfied. My company had a good reputation, and I always did my share of the business.

I started with the company as a sign writer and display man, but there wasn't enough money in it when I came back from the service. I had to make more money, and I told them so. They didn't want me to leave, so they gave me a job selling appliances. I had never sold before, but it turned out that it was much more lucrative.

We had a profit-sharing plan, and I was looking forward to it when I retired. I think I wanted to get out as soon as I could so that I wouldn't have to spend so much time on the hard floors. It was getting harder to get up at 7:30 in the morning, which seemed to me like the middle of the night the last year or so. Actually, it would have been better for me to work until I was 65; the longer you work, the more you gain in the profit-sharing program.

I was hurried in making my retirement decision by the inner-city area where I worked. There was an element of danger involved in leaving the store to go out for lunch, or even to the parking lot. Several members of our department wanted to switch to a store near their homes, but no transfers were allowed. If I could have transferred to a better area, I would have stayed a little longer.

While I was working, I did not worry about retirement. The profit sharing removed a lot of the worry. In normal times, you could have lived a fairly decent life, not too extravagant, but you could have had a good life. The profit sharing was in the form of company stock. I received some dividends from it, but not anywhere near what a normal stock would bring. I was slow in deciding what to do when I retired, and as a result I am kind of trapped now, because the stock dropped in value by 50 percent.

As far as my health was concerned before I retired, the main thing I noticed was that the floor seemed to be getting harder. My legs would ache at night. It was a hard floor, and you had to be on your feet most of the time to produce.

My decision to retire came quite suddenly. My wife and I decided I should retire because of the danger in the neighborhood. Then, in the last year or so before I retired, they were staying open on Sundays, and I refused. The other fellows went along with it. This made it a little tougher on me, because if there was a bad shift they would give it to me. I really hadn't planned on retiring that early.

I had a fair number of outside activities while I was working. I was involved with a local professional football team, with their alumni association; in fact, I am still their historian. I also spent a lot of time at my place of worship doing odd jobs. When you have a couple of boys you become involved in a lot of their hobbies, such as their train setup in the basement. I suppose I made a couple of hundred little houses for the train layout.

Twenty-five years ago, when I was selling appliances, we worked one night a week, and then it was two, and then it crept up to three to keep up with competition. Our shifts were staggered so that you had a little time off in the day, but it didn't give you enough time to do anything. This night work slowed our social activities. When I started working two and three nights a week, it meant that I couldn't spend time with my family like I did when they were growing up.

I didn't plan for my retirement far enough in advance. I thought I would be able to live for a great deal less than what it was costing me when I was working. I didn't realize I would have more time to spend more money, and as a result I suppose that for a few years we spent a bit of our earnings a little too fast. We enjoyed life, and then the realization came upon me that I was going to have to slow down drastically.

We thought a great deal about just doing what we wanted to do every day. I could see the money wasn't going to last as long as I thought it would. Where I made a big mistake was in not reinvesting my stock, and as a result it left me in a tight spot. Had I invested what I had then, it would have worked out fine.

Before I retired, I had a good idea of what I was worth. I thought it would be enough for us to get along nicely, now that the kids are pretty well educated. We had figured out our expenses and thought we were going to be in fairly good shape.

When we made the final decision to retire, I looked forward to it. I was happy about it, and thought that I had worked long enough and had saved enough so that we could enjoy a few years before I got too old. I looked forward to the fact that I would not be strapped down by hours any more. I disliked the idea that I had to punch a clock when I came in to work in the morning, and when I left at the end of the shift. My wife and I decided we would do whatever we wanted to for the first year. I don't know whether you would call it a mistake or not, but as I look back, there are a few things I could have done differently. I should have accepted some of the investment plans that our company offered.

The only major concern I had at the time was financial, related to my son's getting through school. The course he is taking takes ten years. When I left work, he had just graduated from college and had six more years of schooling. I was worried about that because our older boy went through the same education, and I know he needed a little help. It has been a bit of a struggle now to help the second boy. The home we are in, although it is not paid for, is set up so we have nothing to worry about there.

My wife encouraged me to leave for some time before I did. She saw how tired I was getting at work. She influenced me quite a bit. I knew she was thinking of me, and I finally decided to leave.

I didn't plan on a reduced standard of living. I thought I would be able to get along at least the way we had while I was working. I thought it would work out so that we would have a little more time to ourselves and not all the struggle. I thought I had set it up well enough. I made a mistake. I didn't plan on the economy, the inflation, that's what hurt me. I didn't plan far enough ahead. I didn't think my income would be reduced by more than ten or twenty percent when I retired.

My profit-sharing plan was in the form of company stock. I could have sold it all when I retired. I suppose what kept me from selling, or putting the cash into another stock that paid a better dividend, was the tax that I would have to pay. I thought I would go along and cash a few hundred shares of stock each year, but it started going down and I was afraid to do it then because it was only worth half.

The company I worked for sent us a few brochures. When you reach a certain age, they send you retirement planning literature. It was very good, but I didn't take it seriously. When I left my job, some of the retirement groups of the company wanted me to become active with them. They seemed so much older than I was, my wife and I decided we wouldn't have anything in common with them. The first two years, I made no plans at all. My wife and I would get up in the morning, and start out in the car. We had no idea where we would go—we had no specific destination other than doing some "antiquing" and finding a nice place to eat. We traveled around like a couple of nomads for a while, always coming home at night, but we enjoyed it.

Now I spend four to five mornings a week at my temple. My wife joins me in these activities and has found a lot of satisfaction in doing some needed work. I have been referred to as the "artist in residence"; I have hung the pictures and the drapes. I do all the jobs that other people can't get to. I seem to be able to get the work done in a professional way.

There is another hobby I got into five or six years ago which has been very absorbing. I build little models of religious buildings. These have been so well accepted they are now on a national tour. I have been commissioned to do a model of a local fort, the way it was in 1749.

I think everyone should have something to do when they retire. They should be involved. Some of the retirees I have talked to have no fun at all, because all they do is get up in the morning, go for a walk, and read the paper.

My wife and I are both happy about my retirement. The only thing that has been a problem is that I didn't handle my finances too well. If I had, we would be living better now, and we wouldn't have the struggle we do now.

We are now a one-car family, and whatever we do, we do together. We are together all the time. We now go out and have leisurely lunches together; these lunches are about half what it would cost to go out to dinner. I think everybody likes to live a little bit better than they do, and since many of our friends are in a better financial position than we are, it hurts when we have to make excuses that we can't join them. I didn't think I would get to this point when I retired. I thought I would be able to enjoy all these things with our friends, but, now I have to watch it. I don't mind too much, but I worry that my wife is not doing all the things she would like to do.

Since I retired my expenses are lower than when I was working, but my income is lower. The economy has escalated and the stock market has done down, and it has put a hole in my balloon. Everything is higher: food and clothing, the actual maintenance of our home, even the price of gasoline. This is all a big bite.

When I retired, I thought we were making the right decision. When I look back now, there are certain things that I would have done differently. I may have worked another year or two until I was 62. I should have accepted the suggestions in the retirement booklets that the company handed out. I needed financial advice. I didn't spend as much time thinking about retirement as I should have. If I had done more financial planning I think I could have enjoyed my 31 years of work a little more now.

My company didn't offer any retirement help other than the booklets I mentioned. I went up several times to speak to the man in charge and he said that everything was in the booklet. He didn't seem to know any more about it than I did, or if he did he didn't want to make any suggestions. It had to be my own thinking, or what the company booklet offered. If there had been a real company program, where I could have spoken to someone from the company, I think I would be in much better shape now.

CAN PRIOR FINANCIAL PLANNING AVOID A RETIREMENT PITFALL?

Retirement financial planning is necessarily complex. It is clear that unless there is sufficient income to maintain a reasonable standard of living, this will be the most devastating problem in retirement. It is understandable why what appears as a solid financial footing for the future is upset by the failure to consider all sources of income and expenses along with one's style of living.

The impact of inflation by those working and retired is hardly a factor that could be accurately planned for. Most retirees, of varied income levels, expressed their opinion that their expenses would be reduced, but even a moderate lifestyle becomes more costly because of inflation.

This man had a good idea of his net worth, which was heavily weighed by common stock resulting from the profit-sharing. He had considered his general expenses remaining about the same as when he was employed, but his lack of skill in the entire area of financial planning resulted in strapped circumstances. He quickly discovered the pressure of inflation, the needed monies to assist his son's education and an often overlooked area: "I didn't realize I would have more time to spend more money." The decision not to sell his stock at the high point and pay the related taxes well illustrates the jargon of Wall Street: "There are bulls, bears, and pigs."

30

The Pressure of Inflation

Male, 70, married, two children

Education:	high school
Job Status:	bus driver
Retirement Income:	$35,000
Health:	reported good
Retirement Category:	early-voluntary, retired for 14 years

Driving bus was a good living. We didn't want for much. We had what the average working man had. The job was a means to an end; I never thought I was qualified for anything better.

I had looked forward to retirement. Things were getting rough in the city. I was 56 when I left, but I would have stayed to the age of 60 if working conditions had been different.

My problem was with the passengers. They called me vile names, threatened me; I was held up once. On my last day I had a run in with two guys who wouldn't pay their fare. The police arrested them and they threatened to get even with me. That night I turned my bus in and never went back to work.

Things were changing in the city. There wasn't a day when I wouldn't have some kind of incident, the pressure kept building up. The doctor said I had hypertension, and since I've retired I've had no problem, so it must have been the job. It begins to tell on a person when every day they're treated like a dog.

I didn't want to retire until we had the means to build another home and pay for it. The idea of taking a mortgage so late in life did not seem like a good idea. Our social life was in the slow lane because I worked a lot of overtime; six days a week, usually 9 to 10 hours a day. When they put us on five days, I went fishing on Saturdays and had Sundays for the family.

When I thought about retirement I used to think of my dad; he had 30 years of retirement. I figured it was a time where you're your own boss, you don't have to answer to anyone, it seemed pretty nice, but I wanted to be better situated than he was.

My dad was 62 when he retired. He got a pension of $133 a month from the city, and in those years if you had your home paid for you could live on that. He was never under Social Security because city employees did not contribute at that time.

When he retired he bought 25 acres with a nice home on it in the northern part of the state. Taxes at that time were $40 a year but after 15 or 20 years, they went up over $1500 a year, and he was still getting his $133 a month pension. Inflation caught up with him. I didn't want to be in that bind.

We didn't do any planning for retirement. We had thoughts about moving to Florida, but my wife didn't want to go that far away from our children. We never had a budget, but before I retired I figured my net worth—our home and what we had in the bank.

I felt glad to retire. I often thought I'd better be getting once a month, my pension, what I used to get once a week. But, we weren't in debt, we wouldn't want for much, so we'd get by.

We left the big city to get away from the pressures, bought 3½ acres in the country and had a home built. I've been busy ever since cutting the grass, working in the garden and the orchard. My father lived with us for two years before he passed away at 92. We couldn't do any traveling as long as he lived with us.

Retirement has been great; we have had a good 14 years. I think if I knew then what I know now I would have retired a year earlier at 55. As long as I had my 30 years of service in I could have retired at any time, but the longer you stay closer to age 65 the bigger your pension. I kept close track of what my pension would be and when it would finally get up to where I thought we could make it, I retired. Since I've been retired I've stayed ahead of inflation of making some good investments.

I wouldn't say I've had to adjust to anything other than a lot of time on my hands. But our 3½ acres consumes most of the time. We keep busy in spring and summer. Winters are long, but we get away for about six weeks from the middle of February on; that's the only vacation we take.

We just live from day to day. The biggest concern when I wake up in the morning is do I have to weed the garden, mow the grass, spray the trees—there's no end of work. I figured if I could live to be 70 I would have achieved my goal.

WHAT IS YOUR INFLATION STRATEGY?

Inflation—this economic pattern of rising prices—concerns many workers and retirees. It makes little difference whether your pre- or posts-retirement income was high or low, you wonder will your monies cover living costs, your standard of living.

The pressure we feel from this push of prices is one matter when we are working; it is an entirely different affair when we retire. Retirement for most men and women results in a decrease in income, notwithstanding pensions where they are available, Social Security income and private savings programs. The question we must face is what action might we take to avoid financial crisis in retirement.

The strategy of this retiree's conversation offers some guidelines to avoid future financial problems. His firsthand view of his retired father's struggle with inflation was the dominant influence on his retirement plans. Before he retired he had calculated income from his pension fund, Social Security monies and returns on investments. This income, along with a relatively modest lifestyle and a mortgage-free home, he judged would be sufficient to avoid the press of inflation.

No one has the final solution to win the battle of inflation, but the general pattern of this retiree may be helpful in reviewing your own situation. Are you aware of all areas of income, expenses, and have a true picture of your standard of living? If you lack details in these areas some investigation will prove beneficial prior to your retirement.

We all face the fact of inflation. If we develop some strategy to both understand and secure our financial base, we will avoid one of the most disruptive elements in the future.

31

Widowhood and Retirement

Female, 78, widow, one son

Education:	high school
Job Status:	business owner
Retirement Income:	$40,000
Health:	reported good
Retirement Category:	early-voluntary, retired for 17 years

My work was my main interest, but it was really my husband's business. When we got married he wanted me to stay at home, but I told him, "You can't keep me cooped up in a house." So, one day I said, "Honey, I've got something to tell you." He didn't bat an eye, but said, "You were out looking for a job today, weren't you?" I said, "Yes." He said, "Why work for a stranger, work for me." He said I should go back to school to brush up on bookkeeping and then we could work together. That's just what happened.

When the war broke out he decided I would run the business and he would get a job in a factory. We worked that way for four or five years. We put his money in the business and we lived off mine.

After the war my husband said to me, "Do you mind if we put a tool and die shop in the back of the building? I've got a few ideas I'd like to work on." I was agreeable since I had been running the business, and I thought this was a good way for each of us to keep out of each other's hair.

I don't suppose I would ever have retired if my husband had not passed away. He was sick for about four or five years and it was a burden. I was trying to take care of him and run the business. I was ill, but I covered it up. I thought my husband would get worse if he knew about my condition. After he died I went in and had a kidney out.

It really never dawned on me that I would retire, because that was my life. I loved the work. I felt that I was never going to retire, because I had always been active. I don't believe in sitting down—I can't sit still.

When my husband had his first heart attack, I was only about 51 years old. I realized that I ought to do something to prepare for the future. I knew I was going to be left alone. I started my volunteer work about that time in a local hospital. We sold our large house and moved to a smaller one which is just right for me now. What we did was look ahead.

I was not worried about financial matters as far as the future was concerned. My husband had no idea what we were worth. We had always lived within our means; we always paid cash for everything. Money was a tool and that's the way we used it. We wanted to have enough so that I would have no worries for the rest of my life. Now I handle my investments and try to keep within my income.

I didn't have any worries about retirement because I had worked most of my life and I knew there were so many things in the world I wanted to do. It was time to get going and learn—see the world.

The main reason I closed the business was that I would not put up with the unions.

I love retirement. I've gotten into more things. I joined the American Association of Retired Persons, and at the state level I am involved in putting together seminars on aging matters and keeping up with legislation. Some of my friends have asked me why I want to go around with older people in AARP. I find their minds are sharp, and after all, I am an older person.

When my husband died, after I got over a period of grief, I decided that I'm not going to mope, so I had the whole house redecorated. When people asked me if I was going to get married, I told them I could not find a man to fit the decor.

I think a person should plan their whole life. I was raised on a farm and when I was 16 my parents agreed to let me go out in the world. I started on my own and have made my living ever since. When I was a child I would not look at the catalog of children's clothing because I knew that my family could not afford anything—so I kept looking ahead. I kept looking at the women's clothes that I was going to have when I grew up. I was always looking ahead and knowing what I was going to do.

Now, I don't feel as though I am sliding back. You take two steps back and one forward and you keep losing ground. You have to get among people with sharp minds and be on your toes all the time or you are going to lose out.

PREPARATIONS FOR WIDOWHOOD AND RETIREMENT

One subject seldom discussed by married couples when they think of the future years is the death of their partner. This reality is often found to be too sensitive a matter to consider—some people refuse to talk about this eventuality.

The realization of the fact that she would be living alone was clear to this retiree at the age of 51. She and her husband proceeded to look ahead. The preparations for the future included their living arrangements (moving to a smaller house), appreciation of their financial resources (she had handled the finances during their married lives), and a resolve and a determination to be active in retirement. The fact that this woman had for all practical purposes run the family business provided some degree of confidence about facing the future alone. All too often women of her generation have lacked exposure to financial matters—a prime concern about the future years. Her experience about making her way in the world from the age of 16 had prepared her for meeting the world and its demands as well as fulfilling her own needs.

Her preparation for future activities was initiated while she was still working by volunteering in a local hospital. This activity was followed, after the death of her husband, by active participation in the American Association of Retired Persons. This activity provided an opportunity for association with interesting people, as well as afforded a chance to make a contribution to the aging population.

What this retirement experience suggests is the value of "looking ahead." If the years of retirement are to be approached with some degree of confidence and anticipation, either with a partner or alone, considerations of timely future life planning are of major importance.

32

Benefits of Prior Planning

Male, 75, married, 2 children

Education:	college graduate
Job Status:	physician, for 40 years
Retirement Income:	$60,000
Health:	reported fair
Retirement Category:	regular-voluntary, retired for 10 years

Work was my main interest, but I had considered retirement early on, probably after the age of 65. I retired at 65, but this was not my original intention. My plans were to move to California, be semiretired, work two or three days a week. I sold our big home, but, when we were ready to leave my wife backed out. She couldn't leave the family and friends. So, instead of being partially retired, I was forced into complete retirement. I could have gone back into practice at any time. I thought I would try being retired and I found I liked it.

I was successful at my work because it practically satisfied all my needs. There is nothing like the practice of medicine for fulfillment. You are helping yourself, your neighbors, your community and humanity in general. The practice of medicine has changed, more restrictions, more government control, but as far as the enjoyment of the practice of medicine is concerned, it did not change.

My feelings about my work changed a few years before I retired because of my health. I had to cut down on my practice and take it easy because of a heart attack some years ago. Although I maintained my health by diet, exercise and medicine, my condition led to a bypass operation.

While I was working I had a number of interests in music, art, reading, golf and some fishing. This was my recreation and where I could relax.

I usually had time to spend with my friends because I practiced in a group. I had more free time than if I had been in a solo practice.

In the early years there was not much time to spend with my family, but later on this improved. I could spend more time with them because my practice was taken over during weekends, evenings and vacations.

Retirement to me looked like a time of freedom from tensions and work. The practice of medicine is a tough profession. I thought it would be easier, less strenuous and would give me time to follow other interests that I had all my life. Practicing medicine is a full-time job; you can't do it part time.

I guess I've always tried to make plans ahead of time and this was the case three or four years before my retirement. I read many books on financial matters, living arrangements, what to do with my time. As far as legal matters like a will, I've always had one so this wasn't anything new that was done in preparation for retirement.

I had a pretty good idea about my net worth and our expenses. I felt our expenses would remain about the same, but, I couldn't figure out what the effect of inflation would be. I was a bit worried about that; I felt I could make the adjustment if it was necessary.

When I made the decision to retire I was happy about it because I had been looking forward to it for about three years. I immediately began looking for things to keep me busy, occupy my time.

The only major concern I had was the state of my health. I was having some discomfort. I gave up golf because of angina. I learned to take things easy, tried to avoid stress, and tension and to live as relaxed a life as possible.

Before I made the decision to retire I really didn't have much of a discussion with my wife. I think she was concerned about our financial status. As far as she was concerned, I think she would just as soon that I kept working. I don't know if she felt I would be a burden to her, or spend a lot of time around the house. She didn't state specifically what her concerns were.

When I retired we went to Florida for a month on vacation. When we retired I made a number of plans for the future. We would spend three months in California during the winter. I would begin studying subjects that I had been interested in for many years, physics, astrophysics, astronomy, cosmology, philosophy. I attended some lecture series and took a few postgraduate courses in literature, science, arts and science at the local university.

I enjoy retirement. I've never been sorry that I retired. I've been lucky since my bypass surgery; I feel almost completely well.

Really, I haven't had to make any adjustment to retirement, although the financial pressures are increasing in the last couple of years. What with the inflation and a decrease in interest rates, I am getting less return on my investments.

I used to advise my patients, "Don't retire unless you can keep busy full time." I followed my own advice. After having been retired for ten years, I would still give the same advice: keep busy, lots of activity outside the home.

My wife doesn't seem to mind my retirement. During the day she still carries on her own activity and I follow my interests. In the evening we are engaged in the same social activity that we were involved in before my retirement.

I think planning for retirement should consist of making yourself as financially secure as possible. The cost of living is going up all the time and this is something over which you have no control. Also you have no idea how many years you are going to live so you have to anticipate and plan your finances as best you can. If you don't have an interest, or a hobby, cultivate it before you retire.

WHAT ARE YOUR THOUGHTS ABOUT PLANNING FOR THE FUTURE?

Do you remember the days and nights when doctors made house calls? If you recall when the general practitioner, the family doctor, served the needs of most family members, you have a good memory.

Today, with the implementation of increased government supervision of medical services and costs and the rapid rise of malpractice insurance premiums with its attendant effect on the practice of medicine, the close relationship we knew with our doctor is a thing of the past.

Where our former expectation that our doctor would be ever-present to serve our medical needs, this too has changed. The conversation of this physician broadly describes changes in the practice of medicine. It further speaks of his reasons, his plans for the future, similar to others of diverse occupations.

This retiree's rationale for retirement included such issues as changes in the practice of medicine due to more government control, the state of his health, and underlying desire to pursue varied interests he had considered for many years. His decision was made in the face of the fulfillment he realized from his profession, recognizing, however, the full-time nature of his work. Although the time demands were reduced because of his group type practice, retirement beckoned as a time of freedom and reduction of the tensions of his work.

The prior planning for the event of retirement by this physician appears to have contributed to the pleasure he has found, He addressed such subjects as living arrangements, use of his time, and to the best of his ability planned his financial affairs. This combination of important subjects to consider before you retire will contribute in good measure to your satisfaction and pleasure in the years ahead.

33

Relocation in Retirement

Female, 66, married, one child

Education: high school graduate

Job Status: office manager for 21 years

Retirement Income: $25,000

Health: reported good

Retirement Category: early-voluntary, retired for 12 years

My work was rewarding to me. I started doing general office work for about $45 a week and worked myself up to be the office manager. I enjoyed the work over the years. I felt it was a real accomplishment at the end of each month when the books were balanced.

Retirement was something that I looked forward to; in fact that was the plan. My husband and I would work for so many years and then retire. Our plans were speeded up because he had a nervous breakdown. His job was a supervisor of machine repair at one of the local automobile plants and for many months he worked 7 days a week, 12 hour days. He fell apart from the pressures.

When he recovered and went back to work, his employer came out with a retirement plan which basically stated that if you had worked there for 30 years and were 57 years old you could retire. This was a deal we couldn't pass up, so he retired and I continued to work for the next three years.

My husband made himself a garden, which he enjoyed, and worked around the yard. He appeared to be content and was never bored.

Our big activity together was square dancing. Most of our friends through the years have been square dancers. This really constituted the bulk of our activities.

About six years before we both retired we visited some friends in the South. They showed us a piece of property in the mountains which we eventually bought. We had read books about retirement areas and this was one of the recommended spots. We would visit our land on vacations, go square dancing. We had pretty well established friends when we actually moved here.

The deciding reason for my retirement was the sale of our home and property in the midwest. A company had been after us for a year or so and we finally came to an agreement, so I retired. My husband was worried about whether we could make it financially, but we made it fine. When you get into retirement you don't need as much income and your living style changes.

I felt some sadness about leaving the company and people I had worked with, but this was very short lived. Once I made up my mind everything just seemed to fall into place. We moved down south, rented a home until our home in the mountains was built. Our land consisted of 10½ acres in the mountains, with a stream running through it. We lived there for eight years and enjoyed the beauty of our surroundings. Four years ago we decided that our home was more space and more work than we needed, so we sold it and moved into an adult retirement park here in town. Before we had a round trip of 20 miles to buy groceries; now we are just a mile and a half from the shopping mall, a couple of miles from the doctor's office and hospital—everything is very convenient.

We have never had any problems adjusting. We have been very busy and active. You can get as involved as you want in many activities. Our square dancing has been a wonderful activity for both of us. It is something we do together and over the years we have made many wonderful friends—no matter where you go you are never a stranger.

I think when people get to the point of retirement they should check out different places to live and leave the area where they earned their living. If you join a retirement community you will become involved with other retirees and share many activities. Here in our area we have a college providing all kinds of courses; if you are 65 or older the tuition is free.

WHERE DO YOU PLAN TO LIVE WHEN YOU RETIRE?

Thinking of moving out of state when you retire? Perhaps you've dreamed of seeking the solace of small town living, surrounded by a forest and the majesty of mountains. Or does your preference run to the southern shores away from the frost of winter? Whatever your decision of either remaining at home where you have lived and worked most of your life, or relocating, the conversation of this retiree illustrates issues for your consideration.

First, her basic attitude was to change the locale completely from where she and her husband had worked. No mention was made of family ties, roots in the community or any activity which would be missed if they moved to another part of the country. This desire to relocate prompted their investigation of retirement areas, leading to the purchase of land in an area where they had friends.

The six years before she retired provided an ample opportunity to become thoroughly acquainted with the area, develop friendships, participate and enjoy their square dancing activity. The sale of their mountain home after eight years and the move to an adult retirement park to achieve increased accessibility for their needs is another example of their approach to retirement living.

Planning played a prominent role in this couple's selection of where to live when they retired. Their attitude and reasons for relocation were clear, friends were available in the area of their choice, and there were ample opportunities for their square dancing interests as well as others to share with other retirees.

The pattern of this retired couple suggests thorough investigation of a new home site is all important. Would the familiaity of the past, friends, relatives, conveniences be missed? Once these questions are answered, decisions must be made about the new area. Would there be opportunities to make new friends—to find meaningful leisure activities—to have proximity to medical facilities and other required services.

Your decision to relocate in retirement is, in some respects, more critical than any you have made in the past. If you move to another part of the country you will leave whatever social supports you had—friends, relatives—at a time when your dependency needs begin to increase. Further, a major retirement move must necessarily be a mutual decision for many reasons including the probable demise of a spouse.

So while the sunny shores of the South beckon, or the fragrant scent of the Carolina forests are remembered, your practical decision of where to live is significant for your successful retirement.

34

Lifestyle Changes

Never plan on retiring? Don't know how to plan? Turned off by the word retirement? The idea itself is unacceptable to some people because it speaks of coming to the end of the road, that life is over in any worthwhile sense.

Further, for those who reject the idea of retirement, based on their perception of what this period means, retirement planning is out of the question. I propose for our present purpose we discard the word retirement, planning for it, and instead examine lifestyle changes between your working years and when you are no longer employed. This brief, informal approach will indicate similarity and some expected differences between your life today and tomorrow.

The issues you think about today, live with and attempt to handle, embrace financial matters, wellness subjects, leisure activities, family relationships, living arrangements, legal affairs and various adjustment situations. Your success in meeting these challenges and finding solutions, will depend on your ability, determination, and individual situation. Let us compare our lifestyle today with what might be the pattern in the future:

Today

FINANCIAL: Period of increased earning and expenses for necessities and pleasures, a time of investment to increase your nest egg and some savings program.

Tomorrow

FINANCIAL: Period of reduced expenses and income; unless your investment program has been successful, some concern that you are not as secure as you thought due to inflation and higher medical costs.

WELLNESS MATTERS: You are bombarded by all types of nutritional advice; whether you heed these suggestions is an individual affair. Physical exams are recommended on a two- to three-year basis. Your exercise program is promoted to reduce stress and maintain maximum physical and emotional functioning. The demands of your job preclude little daily rest or relaxation.

WELLNESS MATTERS: An alteration in your diet is called for with regard to salt, fat and cholesterol. Physical exams are recommended yearly to assess your overall functioning. Your exercise program might well be modified to a less strenuous pace. The inclusion of some daily rest is recommended if it restores your vitality.

LEISURE ACTIVITIES: The only problem you encounter today is enough time to pursue your interests. Your energy level is high, allowing participation in many activities. You may or may not share activities with your spouse.

LEISURE ACTIVITIES: Time constraints are now a thing of the past. Now the use of time with meaningful activities and the strength to pursue them is all important. Sharing some activities with your spouse is a consideration.

FAMILY RELATIONSHIPS: Between your job and the other roles of spouse, parent, member of the community, you do your best to adjust, to accommodate to your individual relationships.

FAMILY RELATIONSHIPS: The family nest is now shed of children; your spouse continues to work or has retired. Now there is time for delightful companionship or discord.

ADJUSTMENT SITUATIONS: Adjustments during your work life are endless: balancing income with expenses, understanding your children's development, accepting and rejecting the currents of marriage, establishing friendships, coming to terms with your vocational career, and possibly adjusting to being a member of the "sandwich generation" of being a parent and assisting your parents.

ADJUSTMENT SITUATIONS: If you have achieved some success at adjustment resolution while you were employed, the strategies to solve problems are basically the same. The issues are similar: financial stability, recognizing some degree of physical change, constriction of your activities, fewer friendships, enjoying the roles of grandparent status, acknowledging and appreciating the assistance of others as your dependency needs increase.

LIVING ARRANGEMENTS: As part of our mobile society, you may have moved a few times to larger, newer quarters to settle in the suburbs. Your mortgage has increased, but this is part of your lifestyle.

LIVING ARRANGEMENTS: Where are you going to live now that your work life is over? You have options—climate-wise, type of dwelling. Are you and your spouse in agreement? Your present house is paid for—is another mortgage part of your thinking?

LEGAL AFFAIRS: If your personal affairs are in order, you have had a will prepared, probably two if you are married. If your family has increased through the years, as well as your net worth, some estate planning may be called for.

LEGAL AFFAIRS: Is your will up to date as to the beneficiaries of your choice and is it designed to take advantage of current tax laws? Neglect of these matters will result to the disadvantage of all concerned.

The value of knowing where we have been—where we are—and where we are going—provides a foundation of optimism for the future. Our recollections reveal our ability, our involvement to think through, with varying degrees of success, our trials and triumphs. What is important is your awareness of the relationship of the various periods in your life. This idea is expressed by Danish and D'Augelli (1980): "It is necessary to help individuals recognize the similarity among past, present, and future events. The past success experience can help in the present if the individual can make the connection between one event and another."

35

Retirement Insurance

Most of us carry some form of insurance—medical—car—household—life and personal injury. We buy this insurance in the event of, usually, some unplanned happening, so that we are protected against the loss.

What type of insurance do we have to assist us and offer some protection when we think of our retirement?

The policy I suggest carries no premium, is noncancelable, and you have it for life. The name of this retirement insurance is Primary Prevention—a strategy to provide enlightened awareness for your future years.

A pioneer in the field of Primary Prevention, Dr. George W. Albee of the University of Vermont states: "Primary prevention efforts are aimed at persons not yet affected with the condition to be prevented and generally they involve techniques applied to groups, often composed of those at risk for the condition to be prevented" (Albee, 1987).

What does primary prevention have to do with your retirement? If you are considering retirement and are not yet affected by some of the difficulties people encounter when they leave their jobs, you are part of the group at risk. The objective of primary prevention suggests that you take those steps of awareness and planning before you retire to avoid mistakes and miscalculations in your new job-free life.

The issues for you to consider before retirement, under the mantle of Primary Prevention, include: financial: use of time, activities, availability of others; personal: relationships with spouse and important others, living arrangements, health considerations, communication about concerns and goals for the years ahead. If you are reasonably successful in coming to terms with some of these issues before you retire your adjustment and transition to retirement will be achieved more smoothly.

If you have failed to consider some area of importance, or your plans have gone awry, then your approach might well be that of Secondary Prevention.

Secondary Prevention, as defined from a medical viewpoint, states: "Secondary prevention has as its aim shortening the duration, impact, and negative aftereffects of disorder through heavy emphasis on early detection and treatment" (Cowen & Zax, 1967).

One example of something you might have overlooked in your planning for the future involved what your job meant to you. You realize, when you were no longer working, your job had meaning in terms of time, personal achievement, relationships, and your own self-identity. You are feeling some stress sometime after the exhilaration of your newfound freedom has subsided.

Applying the strategy of Secondary Prevention to your problem, you attempt to find those areas of satisfaction, formerly found in your work, in activities which provide meaning and purpose in your life. This is not an easy task, nor is it stress-free. You may find after an exhaustive search that you are unable to duplicate in retirement what your job meant to you. Then, perhaps, the answer is to go back to work, if your health permits, on a full- or part-time basis.

One further approach proposed by Dr. Albee refers to a third level of intervention: " . . . where attempts are made to reduce the incapacities and handicaps produced by serious disturbance, this is called tertiary prevention." This essentially means, as it applies to some specific difficulty you are experiencing in retirement, that you might profitably accept the thesis of tertiary prevention—take whatever appropriate action you can to ameliorate the problem, but accept certain situations which cannot be changed.

The application of the Primary Prevention approach, which I have referred to as retirement insurance, is common sense. Its simple message states that to the degree you become acquainted with the twists and turns your life might take, prior to the event, you will be equipped by your knowledge to plan ahead with some degree of strength and confidence.

V

LEISURE

"I wondered what I was going to do when I retired . . . "
"My only planning for retiring included cultivating my hobby of golf . . . "
" . . . the best thing I can say is to keep busy . . . "
"My major concern was what am I going to do all day . . . "
"I can do what I want . . . "
"You will get old doing nothing . . . "

If you are a planner or approach the events of your life in an unstructured fashion, this pattern describes your personal style or order in the present and future. The previous conversations suggest some degree of planning for retirement, principally financial.

The single issue shared by most retirees reflected their projected plans for their leisure time. Here again, whether the plans were specific or of a happenstance nature, most appeared to have realized satisfaction and the required involvement.

Your selection of activities to occupy and appreciate this newfound abundance of time is a major decision of retirement. Whether you are confounded by the stress of unscheduled time or find fulfillment will present a further challenge to make the most of your remaining years. In any event, retirement is a period of discovery.

The interviews that follow illustrate not only a variety of leisure interests and activities, but the course to discover new pursuits.

36

Leisure Activities in Retirement

We all walk to different drummers when we decide what we will do with our time in retirement. No one can tell us what to do that will provide pleasure and purpose. This necessarily requires an independent decision.

If, for instance, you enjoy making lists—take the cleaning . . . pick up dog food . . . get the car washed . . . cut the grass . . . have your hair done . . . send another toy to your grandchild . . . have someone, anyone clean the basement—then make your list and enjoy yourself. Or if you like watching sports on television, or game shows or soaps, go ahead and have a good time, you have earned it.

The following interviews provide some guidance for our own selection. We see where some leisure interests are a carryover from the retiree's working days, i.e., the "fire-buff" and the golfer. Others—engaged in new interests—discovered pleasurable use of their time in volunteer service; politics; the simple, but joyful, routine of walking in the neighborhood; and pursuing further education in a new field which led to part-time work.

The basis for our choice of leisure activities often relates in a fundamental way, whether we are free or enmeshed in the Chronological Trap.

THE CHRONOLOGICAL TRAP

Have you ever thought about taking flying lessons, bicycling about the United States, going to college for the first or second time, studying the tuba, writing the great American novel, opening that little bookstore you have dreamed about for years, or doing a hundred things you have never done before?

If your answer is yes—wonderful. But if your answer is no, and you are retired, you are still caught in the Chronological Trap.

The Chronological Trap refers to the roles and activities we are expected to play as we live our lives based on our age. For most of us, behavior is specified by others through stages of childhood, adolescence, early adulthood, middle age and older.

The age factor is supposed to dictate and enforce our toilet habits, when we go to school, work, marry, have children, assume and accept a decrease in the quality of our health, and almost when we might reasonably expect to die. This age-related behavior pattern results in our "Chronological Age . . . used as a social marker throughout the life span especially at the earlier and later ends of the age continuum" (Banziger, 1979). We follow the expectations of others, relatives, peers and patterns of our society. We also see ourselves continuing to conform because of our age.

Age is the curse, or trap, some people find themselves in when they retire. Age alone merely signifies one fact—that you have lived so many years. Your age tells us nothing about your vigor, vitality, interests or state of your present health. Further, our age, in no way, suggests that you have reached Piaget's fourth stage of development—problem solving and thinking in the abstract (Piaget, 1952), or Erickson's eighth stage of man—how people view their lives as having meaning and purpose (Erickson, 1975). Finally, your age reveals little of your dreams and hopes for the future.

Certainly, the specific age of 65 has no validity for predicting the human condition: "There seems to be a myth in this country that on one's 65th birthday he is over-the-hill, that his mental faculties leave him, and his body deteriorated. In reality, these processes if they do exist, start long before age 65. Most persons at age 65 are still in good physical condition, and unless hampered by some illness, can compete with younger counterparts" (Tatzman, 1972). Others have reported on the fallacy that retirement is a cause for declining health: " . . . researchers have consistently reported that the event of retirement is not related to health deterioration" (Montgomery and Borgatta, 1986).

One thing we do know—our days are numbered. Since this is the case, then why the rush, the hurry to get the story written today and tomorrow as it was written yesterday?

Your retirement, free from the responsibility of a job, is your opportunity to set your own sails, paint your own patterns of living.

Open that bookstore . . . take tuba lessons . . . start living your dreams . . . that is what retirement is all about.

37

Satisfaction with Leisure Activities

Male, 69, married, 4 children

Education:	high school graduate
Job Status:	cabinet maker, 35 years with equipment manufacturer
Retirement Income:	$35,000
Health:	reported good
Retirement Category:	early-voluntary, retired for 6 years

My father used to say to me, "When you go to work for somebody, you have to work for that person as if you owned the business yourself." This was my attitude about my work. Looking back, I felt I was successful. I found the work interesting because I was doing something different all the time; it wasn't a monotonous factory job.

In the beginning, when I first started, I got along with everyone with whom I worked. Later, when I was more or less in charge, I didn't get along as well because my ideas were different from the younger workers. I had a lot of pride in our work; others were not so particular.

When I was working, I was frightened to death at the thought of retirement. I was really afraid of what the future would hold since I had been an active person all my life. I wondered what I was going to do when I retired; it was a fear of the unknown.

The main thing I thought about was my financial position. I had always been taught that a certain amount had to be put away for the future, and we always managed to do this. I didn't give too much thought to what I was going to do when I retired. My impression of retirement was sitting in front of the television all day long, or sleeping until noon, or doing nothing. But, of course, that was unrealistic.

Six months to a year before I retired we knew we would be financially secure. We planned what our income would be and waited until my wife would be collecting her Social Security. Even though we planned, I still reevaluate our finances every year.

Our major concern had been financial, and when we jumped that hurdle we went on to see what we were going to do with our time. We realized that you can only travel for so long; what would we do when we came home? That worried me.

Ten years before I retired we had moved into an apartment, so I couldn't putter around in the basement, or build things, as I had when we had our home. When we retired, all worry about what we were going to do disappeared. Basically, I think the whole thing has to do with one's attitude. If you say to yourself that you are going to have a good time, you will. If you talk yourself into sitting around and moping, that is what you are going to do.

When we started going to a senior center we had no thought of volunteering, but to attend various programs which we thought would be interesting. I had a problem in the beginning because I felt I was sitting among old people. I did not understand that I felt like a young man walking into this center with these older people, that they were about my age. I found people who were 75 felt the same way. I learned that it's all in your mind. Once you reach this point where you can accept being in this environment, you are more comfortable.

My wife and I were asked to be volunteers at the center. We come in for part of the day five times a week. We are both Medicare advocates, so we discuss the program with anyone interested. I help serve lunches, which is part of a federally subsidized program. We enjoy volunteering, but there comes a time when it seems people take you for granted. My wife and I have discussed this and have decided to cut our time at the center and do some volunteering at a local hospital.

We made a rule, when we retired, to be out of the house by ten o'clock in the morning. If we just go for a walk we get out of the house. My wife takes a day off to clean the house. This is our way of getting out so we won't get stagnated and stay at home.

I think it is a good idea when you retire to set aside a waiting period before you make definite plans as to what you are going to do. Give yourself six months to do all the things you want to do, some of the things you think you are going to be able to do the rest of your life. You will find it becomes monotonous. Then start looking at those things you can do for others.

ARE YOUR LEISURE ACTIVITIES A SOURCE OF SATISFACTION?

How we select our leisure activities in retirement may be some combination of continuing our former interests along with new discoveries—the latter often a happenstance affair.

Some retirees engage in a frenetic involvement as they search for activities to replace their routine of work. This approach often leads to fatigue and frustration and overlooks our principle objective—to find pleasure and personal satisfaction.

Many people state that travel is what they look forward to: This activity is limited necessarily for financial reasons. Others plan on spending more time with their families, but, this area too has its limitations, since most younger family members are involved with living their own lives.

The conversation of this retiree illustrates a successful resolution of leisure interests in retirement. He discovered in an unplanned way, along with his wife, satisfaction in volunteer service at a senior facility. His advice of a waiting period before we make decisions on the use of our leisure time suggests that following purely personal pursuits may not provide the pleasure and satisfaction we anticipated before retirement.

38

Consideration of Retirement Activities

Male, 67, married, three children

Education: high school graduate
Job Status: traveling salesman for 33 years
Retirement Income: $50,000
Health: reported fair
Retirement Category: early-voluntary, retired for 13 years

My work involved selling ladies apparel to retail stores. I traveled on the road about 50,000 miles a year. This job consisted of showing my samples in big and small towns, attempting to maintain good customer relations and getting the manufacturer to serve the needs of the customers. The traveling and selling took all of my energy and attention, but, this wasn't an activity that I enjoyed.

I looked forward to retirement for many years, mainly to get off the road. I tried to plan financially for it as I went along. My retirement came about earlier than I had planned due to a disagreement with my employer. He violated our agreement we had put together when I went to work for him. I did not approve of his methods, which were in violation of our contract, so I retired.

I never worried about retirement. I always felt I wanted to take early retirement because I didn't like the type of work I had to do.

Outside of my work, I enjoyed playing golf, being with my family when I was in town and taking care of the garden. Our social activities were limited. My job involved traveling about thirty weeks a year, so most of my friends were fellow salesmen I met on the road.

My idea of retirement was getting the pressures, the aggravation, the hassle of my business off my back and out of my mind. I looked forward to a much more relaxed daily feeling. I hoped we could do some world traveling.

My only planning for retirement included cultivating my hobby of golf; I've shot par golf for the past fifty years, and structuring my income so I could be independent when I retired. I wanted to be sure our house was paid for before I stopped working and that I didn't have any debts.

After fifteen years on the road, staying in motels and eating in restaurants and leading that type of life, I attempted to go into business for myself. I invested in some small businesses and became a stockbroker at about the same time. I knew it would take time in the brokerage business to make a living, but there were facets of that business that I could not accept. The manager of the office saw to it that you would push the stocks that were on the menu of the company. This disturbed me because I didn't feel I was doing the right thing for my customers and friends to interest them in stocks that were wrong for them. Unfortunately, in two or three years I found that with three children to put through college and parental obligations, I had to go back to the thing I had been successful at—traveling on the road.

My attitude has always been, to build a proper business you had to treat people honestly; you had to think in terms of their best interests. Naturally you had to represent the company you were working for, but the customers were the most important thing I had. I changed lines a few times, but I maintained the same customers because I treated them properly. I think this attitude contributed to my financial success.

The only concern I had about retirement was financial. Through the years I had invested my money prudently in stocks and bonds, but if there was a collapse in those money markets, even though I was conservatively invested, I would really have to worry about money.

When I made my decision to retire, I talked it over with my wife. I thought we could live rather comfortably. We wouldn't be eating at the Ritz every night, but we would be eating well. I told her it was going to be a good future. I am not really sure whether she felt it was a good idea.

I thought our expenses would be less when I retired. When I worked on the road I needed a new car every couple of years; now I put on a lot less mileage, so my car will probably last five to ten years. Now I don't have to spend as much money on clothes, which were a high expense when I was selling.

I've been retired for thirteen years and it has worked out pretty much the way I planned. I've gotten rid of the pressures, the tensions of business. I don't feel that my pulse rate is as high as it used to be because of the aggravations.

My daily routine consists of walking three or five miles, playing golf two to three times a week and taking care of the yard chores. After lunch I generally rest every day. I hoped to play more golf, but I don't find it fun anymore to play when the weather is either too cold or too hot; at best this only occupies four to five hours of the day.

My health has been another story since I retired. I've had a couple of back surgeries, foot surgery, some other problems, but my vital signs are all good. Right now I am recuperating from the foot operation, which is supposed to take from two to six months. As a result I am spending more time reading. Next year, according to my doctor, I'll have to have the same operation on the other foot.

I have decided to resign from the golf club, which is a big decision for me after all these years. For some reason or other, the only friends I had at the club were those in my foursome. One of our group, a man eighty-three years old, has decided to give up the game; we don't have anyone to take his place. My foot problem is, of course, part of my reason for dropping out. When I recover I'll pick up some games at public courses.

I think everybody should have some activities other than sitting in a chair watching television. But, these activities have to be suited to their disposition, their desires. My wife feels that I should be doing something productive like helping humanity, getting involved with community projects. My pleasures are playing with my grandchildren, working around the house, outdoor activities.

My advice to young people is to have some sort of a forced savings plan so that they are putting away money all along the line so they won't have to worry at a later date. I believe you should start to save when you start to work. It is important to develop hobbies, things they like to do that will project into later years, as opposed to field hockey, which they can't do when they are of retirement age.

HAVE YOU WISELY CONSIDERED YOUR RETIREMENT ACTIVITIES?

The challenges of preparing for retirement are many: financial, lifestyle changes, health issues, living arrangements, interpersonal relationships. Your decision about how you will spend your time, staying satisfactorily occupied, is almost of equal importance as your financial planning. The abundance of time in retirement will only have meaning if you give careful consideration to your future activities.

If you have plans for your retirement activities, the following issues may be worth thinking through: Are your interests of a solitary nature, or do you need the participation of others for enjoyment? Have you added to the list of activities you enjoy presently that might well be reduced in the next five to ten years? Are your interests of a seasonal nature, which necessarily prevents full-time participation?

The conversation of this retiree about the pattern of his principal interest, golf, both before and after retirement, illustrates the necessity of considering all aspects of leisure activities. On one hand he suggests the development of hobbies and interests that will project into the later years, as contrasted to "field hockey, which they [young people] can't do when they are of retirement age." But, in actual practice, outside of some family participation and gardening, golf was his principal interest. How this single interest will be affected by his decision to resign from the golf club remains an unanswered question for the present. The significant issue is whether he will satisfactorily replace this activity with something as pleasurable that will also involve interaction with others.

The leisure interest of golf is interesting to examine in terms of retirement. First, as the years pass the golfer may use a golf cart instead of walking the eighteen holes, or may reduce the round to nine holes. If the foursome is reduced for any reason (as was the case of this retiree), might there be others to join the group? Finally, as time goes by the golfer may notice some decrease in skill and stamina, which might dampen the enthusiasm for the game. One matter remains constant—the game is played with others for competition and companionship.

Whatever your interests are for retirement, solitary or requiring social interaction, it is wise to look down the road and expect some inevitable change in others and yourself. If you continually review your plans for retirement activities with some thought to possible changes in circumstances you might profitably expand your interests as the years pass by.

Advantages of
Pre-Retirement Interests

Male, age 70, widower, three children

Education:	college graduate
Job Status:	product cost estimator, 46 years with former employer, an automobile manufacturer
Retirement Income:	$25,000
Health:	reported good
Retirement Category:	early-voluntary, retired for 7 years

I had though about retiring at age 60. When my wife first became ill, we had talked about it. She contracted cancer, and I decided that it would be the worst thing in the world to retire at that time for her sake and mine. She had a five-year battle and I thought it would be better for both of us to have an interest rather than staring at four walls.

My feelings about my work had changed gradually in the three- to five-year period before I retired. I wasn't having fun anymore. I used to enjoy my job and the associations with the people, and I still enjoy seeing some of those same people. Industry was changing. I was having more and more problems selling my programs to management. I come from the old-fashioned school of management; you do a job, take it in, and sell it. The type of work that we were in started with our estimates on a specific body line after the stylists had worked up the job in the styling section with a rendition or proposal. As best we could, we would tell them price-wise whether it would fit in the program they wanted to sell. To most of us, that was an extreme challenge. It usually took a five-year period from the time we started the drawing until we got the automobile on the road. We figured if we came to within two percent, plus or minus, on the estimates, we were doing a pretty good job. We had been as close as one-tenth of a percent on a full model year.

I would come home at night upset. I wasn't fit to live with. The first thing I would do would be go to the cupboard and take out a bottle of Scotch and pour a great big belt. I wouldn't want to eat dinner for a half an hour, until I settled down.

I think it had to do with communication. We would have a deadline to catch on the job; we would be coming along and getting it ready for presentation, then someone would come over from styling, wouldn't like it, change it. Those guys over there were younger than me. They could work all night changing the clay model and they would want us to come along the next day and still meet the same deadline, change all our calculations. It was a frustrating thing. We always took pride in doing a job and doing it right.

I guess part of the problem was that management changed; it was a different type. The business grew through the years and the number of models increased, and we just couldn't be as flexible and turn around as fast as they wanted us to.

In addition to my work, I was interested in the fire service. I am what is known as a "fire buff." It's one of those particular hobbies that you can spend as much time as you want, or as little time as you desire. Right now, it's one hundred percent with me.

At one time I used to play golf, but I wasn't having any fun at that. I started throwing clubs and I decided one day that that's enough of that.

We were a close-knit family. We enjoyed ourselves and had a few personal friends. We were not people who went to the gin mill two or three times a week in order to pass the time. We had more fun at home. I'll admit that at one time, it wasn't financially possible to do it; it took everything we could scrape together to keep this home. I do enjoy travel, but this is involved with my hobby. I go to the important cities, fire-wise, to visit the fire departments. I have no desire even today to visit Europe.

I really never gave retirement a lot of thought, because I knew that if and when I retired, I would be able to keep myself busy. As far as planning in general, I might plan a trip, but to me the closer I got to what I had planned for, the less enthusiasm I had—anticipation is greater than the realization.

I knew pretty well what my financial position was going to be, and I knew primarily what I would be doing. I would be enjoying my hobby and beyond that I didn't have to do any planning.

I retired long before I had to. For about a week I thought, "Just what am I getting upset for, the kids are all raised, they are all in good shape. What am I taking this beating for?"

I walked into the office one day and told the boss, "You are contemplating certain changes that I don't subscribe to. I don't think it's the right thing to do, and as far as I'm concerned, I think we would both be better off if I gave you my letter of resignation and told you that I would like to retire the first of May."

I guess the thing that really got me seriously thinking of retirement was that my company was going to make further changes that I thought, down in my heart, would prevent me from doing the job the way I felt it should be done. I felt if you are going to be in management that you had to believe in the things you were doing. I felt I couldn't take pride in the job any longer. I figured that coming home every night all upset and frustrated just wasn't worth it.

After I made the decision I really had to steel myself for four or five months. The biggest change was a feeling of freedom, a load off my back sort of thing. One of the nice things was that if I woke up in the morning and didn't feel like getting up, I just didn't get up.

If my wife had been living, I would have found retirement more enjoyable. As soon as I retired I went to an international "fire buff" convention. The difference now with my hobby was that I could do it on a 24-hour basis. Before I could only do it four hours a day or at night, maybe work to two or three o'clock in the morning. Now it was my whole life.

My health is better since I retired. One thinks about it, like most people confined to an office all their life, I had chronic constipation. It disappeared.

As far as any recommendations to others who are going to retire or are thinking about it, the best thing that I can say is to keep busy. My advice to young men is to start to develop a hobby early. A hobby doesn't have to be something expensive; it should be something that a person can be vitally interested in and something that they can carry through. People ask me many times about my hobby: "What do you get out of it?" I get personal satisfaction—more important than that, if it hadn't been for my interest in this hobby I would not have had the privilege of meeting some of the finest people. I made friends all over the world and if I got nothing else out of it, it would be the friendship and the reason for visiting many interesting cities.

The main thing I like about retirement is that I can enjoy my hobby at a more leisurely rate. I don't have to crowd it all in the time available, vacation or after work. Now, if a fire alarm comes in any place, I can pick up and go to the fire, watch the fire department, see how they work.

WILL YOUR LEISURE INTERESTS CARRY OVER INTO RETIREMENT?

The rationales for retirement are as varied as those reasons stated for working. People work for a variety of motives: the need to support themselves, for the enjoyment they receive from the association, for the satisfaction and recognition, and because they perceive their work keeps them in the mainstream of life. This combination of work factors is interrelated, but, often a key area is evident which is influential in the decision to retire or to continue working. This retirement profile brings to the fore certain work-related changes which were all important in the decision-making process of retirement.

This man's voluntary early decision to retire, at age 63, was founded on the fact that he found himself out of tune with the new demands of his job. As he admitted, he was "from the old-fashioned school of management," and had difficulty adjusting to the demands for speed and an increased work load. The former challenge of the job, in which he took pride, was no longer realized when he found himself in competition with younger workers. One component of this decision to retire early was related to his understanding of what his hobby of many years had meant to him, and what its future meaning would be. He knew his "fire buff" activities would keep him busy. He valued the many friendships he had made through this interest. There was no question in his mind what would take the place of his former work, or how he would be occupied.

The development of this activity is significant to note from the working to the retired years. While on the job he enjoyed the "fire buff" hobby on a catch-as-catch-can basis, but in retirement it became his whole life. His suggestion to others of finding a hobby—an activity which was not only interesting and absorbing but one that could be continually fol-lowed—suggests this approach as a key to a satisfactory adjustment.

40

The Search for Meaningful Interests

Female, 72, married, two children

Education:	college graduate
Job Status:	politician for 8 years
Retirement Income:	$50,000
Health:	reported good
Retirement Category:	regular-voluntary, retired for 4 years, reelected to county office

One morning when I was reading my mail I noticed some information from the city. I had been a resident for about two and a half years and was not aware of any kind of political activity. I didn't even know where city hall was located. I looked at the faces of the seven people on the city council and said: "Why can't I do that?"

I never had any idea of entering politics, although I had supported candidates in the political scene. I called city hall, talked to a clerk who was surprised by my questions. I asked how does one get to be a city hall person. He explained the procedure of getting petitions signed. I door-knocked and with the help of my family and friends I did all the things you do politically. I got elected and was the top vote getter. There were four incumbents and myself running; I knocked off the council president and that was the beginning of my political career.

I loved my work on the city council. It was something interesting as far as the subject matter was concerned. It covered a whole gambit of areas, social services, business, culture, those were the subjects I was interested in. I had the opportunity to have associations with many people that under other circumstances I would never have met.

This was not a 9-to-5 job. There were many meetings, night meetings, that prohibited me from going to the symphony or meeting with some friends, so I was limited in some areas. You could really make of this job what you wanted. Since I had no other occupation after my husband passed away, I spent more time than a number of other council members working on committees.

Officially, the city council met every week for general meetings, public hearings; on Thursday we had study sessions.

When I retired eight years later, I did so with a feeling of satisfaction that I had done a great job and was appreciated by the people with whom I had worked, the constituents and people in the administration.

My decision was traumatic; the work was still interesting, but I had been on the job for eight years. I thought I could go on to do something else, not knowing what, perhaps spending time traveling and seeing more of my family. I was not involved in the political scene for the next four years. A year before I retired I had a stressful health problem, which I overcame. This may have had something to do with my retiring, but I really didn't think so at the time.

Outside of my work in politics, I was interested in musical culture and was a member of a study group for many years. I was involved with some real estate interests in Florida—all in all I was busy most of the time. My friends called me a gal of many activities.

I knew what retirement would be like because I hadn't started working until I was 59 after my first husband died. Some of my friends with sufficient means do a lot of traveling, others enjoy sailing, and still others spend more time with their grandchildren. I wanted to keep busy doing something that mattered to me.

I think what influenced me about retiring was the campaign. I had gotten tired of the campaign scene, putting up the signs, having the interviews, speaking to people on candidates' night.

My major concern about retiring was what was I going to do all day. I wondered whether I would miss the clout of being in the public eye. You feel some kind of clout, people address you as a council person and you have the opportunity to meet people in the higher political offices. There is something about being in the political eye that is self-gratifying.

I talked over retiring with my husband; he left it totally up to me. I think he would have been pleased whichever way I decided.

During the four years I was retired I got along fine with the activities I had undertaken. I still kept my eyes and ears open for something that might be worthwhile doing; it did not occur to me that I would ever be involved with politics again. My time was taken up with being on a hospital board, my study group, some social activities with my friends and a little traveling.

I think everybody has to have something of interest that they can pursue. If they are happy watching television or going for a walk, or spending time with their spouse, that is perfectly fine.

I reentered politics because a good friend died, who had been a county commissioner. At the funeral someone approached me and asked if I would run for this office. I thought it over for a couple of days and decided it would be a good idea. This was also an elective position, not a full-time job; we meet twice a month, but many of the decisions are made at the many committee meetings.

Now I had a new job to learn. My experience on the city council was helpful in understanding how politics work. I've just been reelected for a second two years and I think I'll retire again at the end of this term. I hope to look around again for some other interesting areas to pursue.

DO YOUR RETIREMENT PLANS INCLUDE PURSUING NEW INTERESTS?

One recommendation to appreciate the newfound time retirement provides is to keep busy. Two interpretations of this advice suggests stay active and occupied in whatever activity fills the leisure time, or choose activities which are personally meaningful.

The life experience of this retiree illustrates a pattern of continual involvement, whether working or retired, with interests that were significant to her. Her political jobs offered structure, interaction with others, opportunities to participate in the political system, and a great source of satisfaction in getting the job accomplished. Likewise, her activities during the four years of retirement were multifaceted—volunteer work, the study group, social affairs and travel.

Underlying her outlook on living, we find a spirit of curiosity, confidence and optimism about whatever the future might hold. If she retires from political office again, it will not be for reasons of disengagement, but rather to explore other interests she might pursue.

The message of this 72-year-old retiree, who returned to part-time work, is simply that our activities are not limited if we have the will to adopt her words, "Why can't I do that?"

41

Appreciation of Freedom in Retirement

Male, 73, married, two children

Education:	college graduate
Job Status:	optometrist for 50 years
Retirement Income:	$25,000
Health:	reported fair
Retirement Category:	regular-voluntary, retired for 3 years

I had never intended to retire. When I was asked at the age of about 65, "When are you going to retire?" I always said when they carry me out. But I changed my mind after a heart attack, which kept me out of the office for about six weeks.

When I went back to the office, I found that work that used to take me an hour was now taking two to three hours. I was putting in about five hours a day, from ten to three, instead of my regular eight to ten hours, but I wasn't getting a great deal done. After I closed my office door at three o'clock, I was still there at least two hours getting the work finished, written up for a laboratory. It was becoming more difficult all the time. I decided that maybe I should quit and enjoy myself a little while I had a chance.

I used to go home very tired at night, something I hadn't noticed before this illness. Little things that had never bothered me before were now annoying, and I figured it was time to get out.

I hadn't given retirement much thought until I became ill. My optometry work was the only type of work I had ever known. I started to work in the laboratories while I was going to school in my spare time. I did that for several years until I became proficient; then I went on to finish school in optometry.

My feelings about my work really hadn't changed too much through the years except that the work was becoming more complicated—government interference, which required certain things to be done that we never had to do before. It seemed big brother was looking at our work and telling us what to do bothered me. I steered clear of a lot of this complication simply by not accepting any government work or government-controlled work, such as Medicaid. I refused to accept that because it entailed a lot of paperwork, and I was able to keep busy without it. Also, there was a certain reluctance on my part to carry all the insurance necessary. It was becoming a fear for us, like the doctors are having today. Everybody was suing everybody. Of course, I've carried malpractice insurance through the years.

As far as my health was concerned, it had been very good through the years, and outside of the occasional cold or being troubled with arthritis, which kept me out of work maybe a week or so at a time, my health had been very good, I hadn't worried about having to retire because of it.

Personally, I had never thought about early retirement. I had seen what effect retirement had had on a brother of mine who retired at the age of 70. I saw him six months later, which was the first time I had found out he had retired, and it seemed to have a bad effect upon him. He was bothered by retirement. He had worked all his life since he was a boy and he was just not cut out for retirement.

My brother had been in various lines of work, men's and women's clothing, tailor, and a furrier. He went through the Depression, and finally had gone into the business of barber and beauty supplies. He was doing very well until he decided to retire at the age of 70, due to the fact that he was having trouble with his salesmen. He decided he would be better off selling them the business, and letting them have the worries, which were eating his heart out. When I saw what happened to him, and realizing his mental condition, I certainly didn't want this to happen to me. I called his son and suggested to him that he give him something to do, send cards out, anything that he might do around the office to pass the time; let him know he had a place to go every day. A bit later I saw my brother and this time he seemed like his old self. He was a different person now that he had a regular place to go. After a few weeks he seemed like he was completely reconditioned. This had quite an effect on me as far as my thinking about retiring.

Our outside activities apart from work through the years was a Saturday night get-together with our old friends of over 40 years, playing pinochle. We led a very quiet life.

I had thought that retirement was fine for those who liked it, those who could accept it. I had a fear that it was a means of sitting down and waiting to die.

I had never done any serious retirement planning because I hadn't expected to retire. I had tried to provide for our older age, but not with retirement particularly in mind. To tell the truth, I would say I had thought more about retiring twenty years ago when I was younger. I had hoped to retire, and I looked forward to retiring at a fairly early age. But as I attained that age, the desire was no longer there.

Through the years we've learned to live very conservatively. I felt that with the help of Social Security, a little income from investments, we could get by pretty much as we had in the past. When I finally decided to retire, I thought it was the best thing for me under the circumstances, that I was not able to continue doing my job as I had been accustomed to. I probably would be better off and feel better if I retired.

I had always been very conscientious in my work. I felt it was getting more difficult to continue to be so conscientious and still do the work. I used to have salesmen coming in from the laboratories; they know how serious I was about my work, and the difficulties I was running into with the laboratory work, getting the work done properly. These salesmen told me: "People don't expect the work that you turn out . . . you are a throwback from the old days . . . you are the last of the old-timers that demand quality work . . . it can't be done. . . . "

Today everything is speed, speed . . . turn out more work, regardless of quality. I found I was sending back so much of the work to be redone that there were times I couldn't get anything delivered. I saw myself starting to let little things slide by that I would never have accepted previously.

My wife thought my retiring would be good for me. She figured I had enough, and I was getting to the point where small things bothered me more than they had in previous years. I have been very fortunate because my wife has been in my office as my receptionist for the last 14 years.

I figured when I retired that I would have a reduced standard of living, probably a third to a half, but I knew where the monies were going to come from before I retired. Also, I thought my general expenses would be a little less; of course, I didn't know that conditions were going to change as much as they have as far as inflation. I thought that I might have to spend a small amount of my principal besides my income to get along.

I didn't have any real immediate plans after retiring. I just took things easy. I stay home and make the most out of every day as it comes. As far as the last three years are concerned, I love it. Love every day and enjoy it. My health is better at this time than it was three years ago. I have fully recovered. I walk several miles every day, and during the summer I do not need any medication. During the winter, I take medication because of the cold and the winds.

All in all, I have adjusted very well. I do not miss my work. My wife says that she does, but I am very happy in retirement. As far as my general activities, I sleep very late in the morning, until nine o'clock. After breakfast, dressing, I go for a walk if the weather permits. The only thing that keeps me home is rain or a heavy snowstorm. I walk in the coldest weather. I was cooped up in an office for 50 years and now it is just like being out of jail, out of prison, now that I know what it is to walk out the door any time I want to go for a walk. I enjoy meeting people on my rounds of walking and talking to them. Children get to know me and speak to me. The dogs all know me, and learn to come to me or bark at me as the case may be, and I enjoy all of this.

Our social life has changed since my retirement. We have discontinued our Saturday night get-togethers because many of our friends have passed away.

Retirement has been wonderful for me. I think the answer is if you can keep busy, it doesn't matter what you do as long as you keep busy, walking, reading, anything that will occupy your time so that you just don't sit and think about or worry about yourself. This is all that is necessary to be happy. You don't need a lot of money. I think the first thing I found out about retiring is that my time is now my own. I am free. I can do what I want, when I want, with no obligations, no ties to anything or anybody. We make our plans from day to day.

I don't really believe that I had to get used to retirement. I seemed to drift into it and immediately enjoy it. Just the fact that I didn't have to get up at seven o'clock in the morning and rush to get ready for the office was a great relief.

WILL YOUR RETIREMENT PROVIDE A NEW ROUTINE FOR LIVING?

We are all, to some degree, creatures of habit. We shop, pay our bills, do our banking, engage in social activities following some fixed routine.

This habit pattern reflects our personality and attitude toward the way we live our lives.

When we consider retirement we reflect on what our life pattern of work has been. This sometimes forms the foundation for an attitude of anticipation or rejection of the event of retirement.

This retiree, after some 50 years in his chosen field, had a predisposition against retirement. Not only was his lengthy work pattern an integral part of his life, but he subscribed to the myth that retirement "was a means of sitting down and waiting to die." Further, he had witnessed the maladjustment of his brother when he stopped working, which contributed in some measure to his concern about retirement.

Old habits are hard to break, but the event of a heart attack combined with the pace and disregard for quality work resulted in a decision to retire. For the first time in his life he followed a new routine . . . staying at home, sleeping late, enjoying walks in the neighborhood, and reveling in the fact that time was his own.

What this retiree's experience makes clear is that our habits and routines are subject to change. Where what was appropriate and self-satisfying at one point in a person's life may take a new direction offering opportunities for new experience and pleasure in retirement.

Thoughts on a Second Career

Male, 68, single

Education:	college graduate
Job Status:	material handler, 21 years with a health institution
Retirement Income:	$20,000
Health:	reported good
Retirement Category:	regular-voluntary, retired for 3 years, returned to part-time work

My work was my life, but I wasn't satisfied because I was working beneath my educational qualifications. I knew the job when I started because of my army experience. I had the idea I was going to move up, but when they found that I was so qualified they wouldn't permit me to move up.

I found out about this when a lady came to our business school during Career Day. She told us about a giant in the health care field and led everyone to believe you could move up the ladder. I thought this would be a good place to start, so I applied for the job.

The first thing I discovered was that they were not hiring anybody over 40 years old. I was 42 at the time. They told me their reasons; most people that age can't work very long, they get sick, they definitely don't like young supervisors, they already have had their minds made up on how they are going to do the job, regardless of what they are told, and they just didn't like that age people.

I asked, "Do you think there's anybody in the world who could do this job, get along with supervisors and coworkers?" The personnel lady said,

"Oh, yes, somewhere in the world there is somebody who can do it." I said, "I'll make a bargain with you. Give me the job; I'll work a month. If I find I can't do what you want me to do, I can't get along with people, I can't learn, the job is too much for me, I'll come back and tell you." I got the job and worked there for 21 years.

After I had been there a while I learned that you can bid for other job openings. There was a job in the accounting department, and since I had some experience from the army, I applied. The system was that you apply for the job, have an interview, take a test. If they find you are qualified, you get a release from the department you are in, and then you are transferred.

My department head refused to give me a release. He said, "No, I can't let you go, you're one of the best men I've got." I tried going to administration—that's the way things worked in the army—but I failed there. They told me, "You'd better stay where you are; you are contributing a great deal to the organization."

I had looked forward to retirement, but not at that time. At 65, I felt I could work as long as I felt good; when I didn't feel good, I would retire.

My feelings toward the job changed a few years before I retired. They started a management engineering department; it's a misnomer, it has nothing to do with engineering. It's a time study group, They come around to the job, do a time study, and that's alright because some procedures might be old, outdated, and they might come up with some good ideas. But, in my department, we had an internal time study going on all the time, because it was a production type of work. So much had to be done in a certain amount of hours every day, so we had to time-study ourselves to make sure the job was done in the most feasible manner. We knew how the work must be done; this came from years and years of doing the work.

When these young fellows came in, right out of high school, into college and into this work, they didn't know anything about the job. The administration told us, "You have to cooperate with these guys, listen to them; they are under contract, all they have to do is put in a bad word and you'll be fired."

We tried to go along with them, but some of the things they came up with were ridiculous. I wasn't going along with it, but my problem came up from a supervisor, who seemed to feel their suggestions were right. When discussions came up he said to me, "You're getting too old, your brain has stagnated, you are not susceptible to new ideas."

The plan the time-study people had was based on a machine: A machine would grind out 360 pieces of material every hour. People don't work that way, one hour they might handle 360 pieces, the next hour 355 or 370. They set up a production schedule related to your pay. If you were short you could lose an hour's pay, but if you got ahead you didn't make any extra money.

I had thought that the older you get, not in age but in years of seniority, the less heavy work you would have to do. I found out to my dismay that you were supposed to get out the same amount of work after 20 years that you got out in the first year.

I didn't worry about retirement. I knew I would never starve. I thought about retirement when I was 65, but I knew people who were still working at 75 and 80, and I couldn't understand why I couldn't work that long.

My health became a factor about three years before I retired. As the result of an operation, the doctor gave me a "light duty" slip. When I returned to work, I showed it to my supervisor. He said, "We have no light duty work for you, so the best we can do for you is to let you go." I knew for a fact that there were numerous places where I could have worked; there were people who would have liked to have me in their departments.

I refused to go, and instead went out and got a lawyer. Under the Fair Employment Practices Law, it states that you can't fire a person unless you first find out that he can't do anything for your company. My experience was both good and bad; everyone will tell you that you can't win over management and stay. When the word got out that I was being released from my department, seventeen departments wanted me. But I didn't want to change to another department. The administration told my department head, "If you let him go, you cannot request another man to fill his slot. If you don't need him, then you don't need anybody else!" When my supervisor found out that he would lose a work slot, he decided to let me stay.

We all talked about retirement in the shop; nothing serious was discussed. I never thought about it.

I never had any interests other than my work. I lived my job. I went to work and I went home, week after week. We have a lot of people who do this, and I found out it is a detriment. I loved taking care of the patients, supplying the nurses with their needs. Once in a while I'd get a pat on the back; I felt good about it because somebody was pleased.

When I thought about retirement I envisioned it as sitting on the porch in a rocking chair, reading the paper, watching TV. It was an absolute leisure life, you did what you wanted to, or you didn't have to do anything at all. You never thought you were going to have any bills; you forgot about that.

When I made the decision to retire I felt happy. I realized that I was never going to get anywhere with those management engineers, or my department head. I felt the longer I stayed, the worse the situation would become; and if I stayed too long, I might get fired.

I had no major concerns about retiring. The only thing I thought about was where I was going to live—in Chicago, Detroit, Atlanta, or Denver. I never planned on a reduced standard of living, because I knew I could live the way I was living.

I talked over the idea of retiring with some of my friends, since I don't have any family. They told me the best thing they had ever done was to retire; they didn't see any reason why I shouldn't do the same thing. They said, "There is no reason to stay there and go through a hassle every day. After all the years you've spent there, the dedication you've put in, and the way you've been treated, come on out."

When I made the decision to retire I put in for my retirement pension and for my Social Security. About that time the travel people start talking about signing up for the travel club. My organization had the inside track, so they talked to me every day about signing up. They tried to get you in the mood; so, after I retired, I realized that I had nothing to do, and I signed up. It was nice—fly now and pay later. It was wonderful; you can go anywhere.

Retirement is a state where you have to make something happen. You no longer have bosses to tell you to get up, or tell you what to do. You have to be your own boss and make yourself do things; this is a retiree's life.

One thing I found out in a hurry was that waiting 30 days for a check was different than getting paid every Friday. When I was working I could borrow money and pay everybody back on Friday. But when I realized that I had 30 days to wait for my checks, I would have to keep on borrowing.

Most retired people get their pension check in the first month; it took me three months to get my first check, and I had to wait a month before the first Social Security check came along.

When I retired I found out there are hundreds of retiree organizations. They come around and invite you to attend meetings. I discovered there was a whole new world of activities open for retirees.

I joined an organization called Seniors Helping Seniors. There you are dealing with everybody your same age. The jobs are listed and you pick out what you want to do. My first job was driving a car delivering prescription medicine to invalid senior citizens. The first day we went to 14 drug stores, picked up 87 prescriptions and delivered them.

My advice to anyone thinking about retirement is try to stay busy. You will get old doing nothing. Try to start any type of hobby, do something rather than sitting around the house—you will rot.

The first year wasn't rough, but I found out that I was going to have to do something. I got tired of traveling, and I knew I didn't want to go back to work. It seems after working so long you get regimented and you have to remember you are not working anymore. You wonder why you have so much time that you never had before.

Most of my friends are other retirees; we have a little retirement group. You learn when you retire to make friends of your retirement buddies.

I think it's a good idea to have a nest egg before you retire. If you plan to retire at 65, you should start your planning at 55 so you have ten years to work on it. The main thing is time. You've got to plan what you're going to do with your time. Time will kill you. You have so much of it, and you don't know what to do with it.

I went back to work as a result of going to school. I decided to go to school to study computer programming, not to get a job but just to fill up my time. When I completed the nine-month course, I showed my certificate to a secretary in a local social work agency. Her boss asked me if I wanted a job; I declined and told him I went to school just to be going. He asked me, "Well, why don't you give us a hand until I can find somebody?" I said, "Okay, I'll give you a hand for a little while." I've been there for three years.

I work part time and this is what I like about the job. I make my own hours, about 20 to 25 hours a week. I took the job to help this man. I firmly believed I would not be there more than a month. I fell in love with the people I was working with and I've always had a strong desire to help people. I get so much joy out of seeing the eyes of people light up when you do something for them.

I felt different when I went back to work. I had something to look forward to, the weekends were different because I had planned what I was going to do on Saturday and Sunday. I might work another two years; I'll be 70 then, and I don't know whether it would be advisable for a 70-year-old man to work a computer. I'll have to see.

THINKING OF A SECOND CAREER?

The option of going back to work after you retire, on a part- or full-time basis, will depend on a variety of reasons. These include financial need, additional discretionary income, an opportunity to continue your involvement and pursue your dreams and the use of your time.

Some men and women require additional income to supplement their regular sources—Social Security, pensions, savings plans—due to inflation, inadequate financial planning and unplanned-for emergencies.

Others, although no real financial need exists, would appreciate additional monies for unbudgeted pleasures, purchases, extended travel.

Some retirees consider a second career as an opportunity to realize their dreams: open a small bookstore . . . operate a bed and breakfast inn . . . become a consultant in the area of their former work . . . bake and sell cheesecake that friends have raved about for years.

The matter of time—the use of the many hours in retirement—is a concern of many thinking about retirement and a source of difficulty for some retirees. The development of a second career, although unplanned, is illustrated by the conversation of this retiree. As he expressed his feelings a year after retiring, "You wonder why you have so much time that you never had before." His decision to attend a computer school to "fill up my time" was clearly not job related. He stated that he had no intention of going back to work. However, the job offer, which he accepted, evidently fulfilled some of his need to be involved.

There are four areas you might consider before making the decision to go back to work. They include personal affairs, the required financial investment, your health, and the hours necessary to achieve some measure of success.

If you are married, would your decision to start a second career be acceptable to your spouse? What is your reason—additional income, need for work involvement, motivated to be your own boss? Whatever your rationale, sharing your thoughts and feelings about a second career will assist your spouse in understanding this new interest.

Would your second career choice involve a sizable financial investment? The possibility of gain or loss must be recognized once you have achieved a solid financial footing in retirement.

If you are in good health when you retire, you are aware of some inevitable change due to normal aging down the road. The prospect of being your own boss is, no doubt, exciting, but have you considered the amount of time you would have to spend to make your new effort worthwhile?

These issues are suggested for your review in thinking about a second career, so that once resolved, you are confident about returning to the world of work.

43

Volunteering

One activity which is enjoyed by a growing number of retirees is that of volunteering. Volunteering may be defined in different ways—offering to help others—working without payment. A broad definition of this service is described by Jacqueline Washington, recipient of the Sojourner Truth Award for outstanding businesswoman of the year in 1982 by the National Association of Negro Business and Professional Women: "Volunteering is the rent I pay for the space I occupy on this earth."

The following true story illustrates some of the components of the volunteering experience.

A male volunteer elected to spend his time talking to patients and family members in the radiation-oncology center of a local hospital. There was no particular orientation for this type of service. The volunteer believed the mere presence in a hospital setting was felt as a threatening environment by the support team, the family, and certainly by the patient. He considered his job was to reduce some of the tension and anxiety in whatever manner this could be achieved.

He talked to patients on a variety of subjects, his dog, gardening, farming, sports, cooking and whatever special interest he could glean from their conversations. When everything else failed, they would talk about the weather . . . how hot or cold it was . . . when were we going to get some rain. Such subjects as how many radiation or chemotherapy treatments the patient had to take, or his or her struggle to survive, both physically and emotionally, were not mentioned.

The volunteer attempted to communicate with all patients in some form: by a greeting, providing a magazine or an additional blanket or pillow, or a few quiet words of encouragement: "Hang in there." Communication with the staff aides and nurses was also part of his effort, to pass on the needs of patients relative to any discomfort. The staff appreciated the volunteer's assistance because doctors and nurses were often too rushed for everyday small talk, yet they realized the value of it from the standpoint of the patients' feelings. This interaction by the volunteer and staff was viewed as doubly important, because under their hospital garb, they were people feeling their own stresses and strains of their jobs and personal life. The job of this volunteer was multifaceted— first the patient—then the family—finally the staff.

One day the volunteer talked to a patient sitting in a wheelchair waiting for her radiation treatment. Their conversation got around to the subject of a good recipe for meatloaf. She offered her recipe, which the volunteer wrote down. She stated in all honesty, "I have not cooked anything in 15 years."

Later that day the volunteer purchased all the necessary ingredients, baked the meatloaf and the results were wonderful. He decided that some effort should be made to thank the patient. He bought a "Certificate of Appreciation," typed in the appropriate information and had it presented to the patient.

This story is actually my own; I was the volunteer. On September 14, 1988, my birthday, I was presented with the following letter:

Dear Richard,

I am impressed! Also, proud, pleased and delighted to receive the award.

You are one of those rare and unique people who still believes in "follow thru." That's nice.

I wanted to take a minute to thank you, as I had just arrived for my treatment and to check in to the hospital for chemotherapy. So you can see, Richard, the award was a bright star in otherwise not too exceptional day.

Stop by for a visit if you have time. I'm in room . . . and will be here for a few days.

Sincerely,

(Patient's name withheld)

What can be learned from this story of volunteering in retirement? Volunteering provides opportunity for human interaction and face-to-face, eye-to-eye contact with people in need of help. Whatever service you perform, they are endless in variety and you receive the joy of just payment. Being a volunteer on a regular basis provides some degree of structure in your life—something to look forward to every week. The fact that you are with people often not as fortunate as you can provide a broader perspective of your community.

If you are satisfied merely to fill a morning or a day a week without particular regard to the activity, then your needs will be met. On the other hand, if your mission as a volunteer is to provide a human service with some quiet often nonverbal expression of understanding by the recipient, it is important to be selective. Volunteering offers many rewards when the right mix of person and activity is achieved.

If, after you retire, you experience feelings of loss, some service to others may reestablish your sense of self-worth. The interaction with others which you enjoyed while you were working may be found in many volunteer activities.

The how's, why's, and where's of volunteering are published in a booklet titled "To Serve Not To Be Served," by the American Association of Retired Persons, 1909 K Street, N.W., Washington, DC 20049. You will find this publication informative as to the many types of activity in which you may participate.

One final word about volunteering. This is an activity where your payment, your approval by others, in the usual sense, is often missing. Do not expect to see your picture in the daily newspaper or look forward to appearing on television to talk of your worthwhile service. Your voluntary service may be acknowledged by a pin or letter of appreciation stating your interest and hours worked. Your reward for whatever form of human service you perform will be seen in the eyes of those you serve. If you feel the true calling of volunteering, giving and receiving, you will humbly accept the silent blessings of those you serve.

44

My Story . . .

Note: Friends and others interested in my effort to understand retirement strongly suggested I include my own experience. The following is a self-interview of my personal past and continuing effort for eight years to cope with the pleasures and problems of retirement. Fundamentally, I have answered many of the questions and responded to the issues raised with all retirees.

Male, 68, married, one child

Education:	college graduate
Job Status:	automobile dealer
Retirement Income:	$60,000
Health:	reported good
Retirement Category:	early-voluntary, retired for 8 years

My feelings about my last job were quite the same as all previous jobs—do your best, be conscientious. I suppose my generation never thought too much about the quality of their work life. You went to work fundamentally for the money to support yourself, and if you were successful and also liked your work you were doubly blessed. The money was a means to an end, but I really didn't have much of an idea what the end was going to be.

For many years I was interested in the work. When I joined the dealership I had no experience with selling or servicing automobiles. This was a period of learning and gradually assuming greater responsibility. My success and satisfaction with the work was the result of good acceptance of the product by the public, increasing owner satisfaction with our operation and by and large a team of people who worked well together. However, I was not a born "horse-trader" who enjoyed the bargaining back and forth between the customer and the salesperson. My talent in this area was limited because I wouldn't or couldn't adjust my sales approach to the different personalities that came along to buy a car.

My approach to the people I worked with, however, was considerably different than my contact with retail buyers. In a word, my management style was simply that, but for the grace of God, I would be the porter instead of the dealer, and would have appreciated being treated in a humane fashion. It really doesn't take people a long time to discover if you are interested in them as people and fellow employees. There were many occasions of birth, sickness, death and celebrations where I appreciated the opportunity to share and participate in a small way in the lives of people on whom I depended,

I suppose I had looked forward to the idea of retiring, but this was not based on any particular expectation other than that the pressure and responsibility of running a small business would be over. Somewhat related to the idea of retiring someday, I kept track of the growth of my nest egg on a yearly basis.

My feelings about my work had changed for a variety of reasons about three years before I retired. A reasonable profit was gradually getting more difficult to achieve, and since we were a small dealership we could not operate on a volume basis. The price of our cars was increasing yearly and as a result, people traded cars less often and we were losing some of our longtime customers. Perhaps because I was getting older, I had less patience with some of our temperamental employees—often these are the most highly skilled and difficult to replace. I wondered about my management style, perhaps the business was being operated too much like a family instead of being run in a straight business-like atmosphere. And after all the years of attending dealer meetings, where relatively little was accomplished, I was fatigued.

While I was working I had no worry about retirement because, in truth, I had little understanding personally about what changes were to occur.

My health had been good through the years and had nothing to do with any thoughts about retirement.

During the years I was working I had no particular thoughts about early retirement or retirement in general. I had calculated on a yearly basis my general financial position compared to our expenses, so I was aware when I might be able to stop working.

Prior to my retirement I had a number of varied interests. I studied the clarinet, swam at the Y's pool, had a morning exercise program and attended to financial matters of bill paying and financial investments. Other activities included working at my office at Wayne State University, visiting and assisting my aging mother, miscellaneous readings of psychological journals and work on retirement research. Some of the pleasant times involved were some social activities of breakfast and lunch with a few friends as well as a night or two out of the house with my wife. I have noted through the years, not only what my activities were, but, I rated them as to things I must do and things I really enjoyed doing. Interestingly enough, the change and reduction in these activities had an important bearing on my adjustment to retirement.

My work never interfered in any way with available time to enjoy the company or my friends and family. I've always contended, even in the busiest periods of my life, there was always time to relate to the interest and needs of others.

While I was employed my thoughts on retirement, to the extent I gave the matter any specific consideration, were that my life would be a new ballgame—mainly a relief from the various responsibilities of running a business, the sales, the profits, the personnel, relations with the factory— the latter two areas for some years presented some degree of frustration.

Generally speaking, I have always been a planner of business affairs, not personal planning. I don't think I engaged in any specific planning for retirement, other than to be quite accurate through the years as to my financial position.

On such matters as health and nutrition: I am about fifteen pounds overweight and I smoke. I hope to reduce the former and eliminate the latter.

On living arrangements, we have lived in our suburban home for thirty-odd years, have pleasant neighbors, a garden to gladden the eye, a fenced yard for my dog, and have no plans to move. In the backyard are two of my favorite trees I planted many years ago, a sun-burst locust and a mountain ash; if we moved I would miss them as trusted friends.

We have finally solved the bird-feeding problem, not a minor matter. We purchased a metal bird feeder through the National Audubon Society, which thwarts all efforts of squirrels and pigeons. When they land on the feeding platform, it closes, thereby making it possible for only small birds, or perhaps one blue jay at a time, to have breakfast.

Through the years we have added to the house a couple of times, the most recent of which was the kitchen so my wife has endless room to create her own outstanding pastries.

We have taken care of our legal affairs—two wills, and our estate planning is up to date.

No particular attention was paid to what my leisure activities would be in retirement because the use of time in the past had never been a problem. Relative to any particular activities with my wife, I have never considered this aspect, since she was usually satisfactorily involved with her own interests. She is a more social person than I am, and enjoys the company of a lot of people, so, as a result we shared few activities together.

As far as any thought of going back to work in terms of a second career, that was the furthest thing from my mind.

When I began to think of selling my business and retiring my thoughts were all positive. Two matters were clear: Financially there should be no problem to generally maintain the comparatively modest standard of living we had enjoyed for many years. Secondly, it appeared the business was going downhill. We were surviving, in large part, on profits from the past—so it was largely a business judgment that encouraged my thoughts.

Before I made the final decision, I had no concerns about the future. Naturally one hopes that the body machine continues to operate in fair fashion, but in general, there were no thoughts or considerations about my aging or anything else.

I did not discuss the idea with my wife of selling my business and retiring. Since this was mainly a business-related option, I figured I was in the best position to understand what was involved. We had no discussion or communication on changes that might result in such things as to what I would to with my time, or what activities we might share together.

Before I retired, as discussed in Chapter I, my sources of information about retirement were extensive—research—seminars—the literature— interviews with retirees. So, in one sense, I was aware of the circumstances one encounters in retirement. But, I obviously did not, or could not, relate what I had learned to my upcoming life changes. Perhaps this is not unusual in that for some of the crisis of living (by crisis I mean a shift in direction), one must experience these turning points personally to appreciate their broader meaning.

I have not been employed for eight years, except one year as a part-time staff member of a nursing home as the new resident counselor. I have concluded that for me retirement has been a mixed bag of feelings. In fact, as I write these lines, in all honesty I am still making an effort to cope in a meaningful fashion. I think the key to my difficulty and approach to a successful adjustment relates to the word meaningful. I do not find fulfillment in cards, golf, most spectator sports, any quantity of TV, travel and social activities. My interests appear to lie in more solitary pursuits—bird-feeding—gardening—listening to music—farming chores of planting corn—riding the tractor as I cut the grass. I enjoy walking the woods in all seasons, noting the continual change of sights and sounds. As far as people are concerned, I do enjoy conversations on a one-to-one basis.

My adjustment problems certainly did not surface in the first year of my retirement. The feeling of euphoria, the joy of the fullness of time was appreciated—no pressure, no business or personal problems, no sameness after thirty years and the lift from the shoulders and spirit of responsibility. My particular and somewhat ongoing problems of adjustment developed after the first year.

How I have planned my time and activities continues to develop in changing patterns. As I mentioned previously, my activities prior to retirement were numerous and varied; since retirement a major reduction has taken place.

If I have any recommendations to others about the nature of their retirement activities, I suggest try to figure out what you really like to do, what brings you fun, pleasure and satisfaction. This is a difficult job. To know oneself at age fifty is often quite a different affair from age sixty, seventy or eighty. Our aging, our likes and dislikes change, and the availability of important others and friends plays a part in how we spend our time.

Now, to some of my adjustment problems. A year after I retired my mother passed away so that the time devoted to her needs was available for other pursuits. For various reasons other activities were dropped, the music study, the swimming program, interest in psychological journals. The season was fall, the farming play-chores were over, the wood had been cut for winter. I encountered days without plans. It was a structureless time. I again felt the fullness of time, but, now it was not rich in meaning. There were no thoughts at this time whether I had made a mistake in retiring—the pleasure and joy of the relief from work responsibility was still appreciated. But, I felt unrequited, unfulfilled in terms of a portion of my time.

There was one incident that at the time I did not consider a significant cause for my feelings of lethargy, lack of interests and motivation. The details are, briefly: I applied in the spring of 1981, at the age of 61, to two local universities for admission to their graduate schools to further my education in the clinical side of psychology or in educational psychology. Prior to applying I had presented to the interviewing parties at both institutions my various publications. It was my belief that my accomplishment in terms of publications would illustrate that I was on my way to contributing to the needs of society in the field of retirement education.

I was declined entrance to both universities. This was to be my first experience with being rejected because of my age. I was more upset than I realized. It was unlikely that other applicants had presented as many proven examples of their work and subconsciously I felt let down. On the other hand, I realized that a motivated 24-year-old had many years to make his or her mark in the fields of psychology or education.

It was approximately at this time I began volunteering two mornings a week at a local hospital in the CAT scan and radiology departments. Although I had a "people interest" much of my life, I was surprised and pleased to discover how much I felt at home in these surroundings. For the next four years I learned in my interactions with patients and family the quiet chemistry which develops between the volunteer and those in need of medical attention.

My wife's feelings about my retirement were concerned that I did not have enough to keep me busy and appeared to have little to do that I truly enjoyed. She was correct: At the time I did not understand some of the mild stress and feelings of dislocation I was experiencing.

I have never missed the regularity of a work schedule, but I came to realize that I needed some structure in my life, not necessarily on a daily basis. I would not take a full-time job because at this stage in life I do not need any locked-in feeling of the burden of responsibility. Now my present volunteer activities in a hospital, my assignment to the Institute of Gerontology at Wayne State University, visits to the farm, readings on retirement and interviews with retirees provides a full schedule and structure. A recent development, my wife's participation in both the garden and home and her enthusiasm to plant and pick the variety of sweet corn she prefers, has provided us with a shared activity we both enjoy.

If I had it to do all over again, I would not have retired earlier. As I mentioned, my decision to retire was a coming together with what seemed like an appropriate time to sell my business and relief from the pressures. Prior to that time, I worked on a daily basis, running the ship to the best of my ability, but calculating yearly the state of my finances with some anticipation of not working in the future.

If I have any recommendations to others about specifically planning for their retirement, it would be to attempt to be aware of specific changes which might occur when the routine of your work life is over. I think the best way to achieve this is to take a detailed look at your life while you were working. Some matters to consider are the following: time, what your job means to you, other than the paycheck, relationships, present activities, getting your house in order, legal affairs, and some look ahead to your future living.

Retirement Revisited

The retirees have spoken. Now that we have traveled their road of retirement, let us continue our journey.

It was fall again. The summer's corn crop was excellent, the drought notwithstanding, thanks to the great gardener in the sky. Swimming in the farm pond, cooled by underground springs, helped us survive the heat of the summer. Now I begin my eighth year of retirement.

My years have been spent, in part, listening to others tell their stories of retirement. I have arrived at a better understanding of this turning point in my life. If you are puzzled by the diversity of attitudes expressed by the retirees who shared their lives with us, let us agree it was a mixed bag of anticipation, avoidance or lack of interest about the event of retirement.

One day a 58-year-old lady was mandatorily retired—fired in the old-fashioned sense. On another day a man elected regular retirement at 70. Most retirees stated they were not in favor of early retirement; yet, the majority chose the option of early retirement. The majority said they had engaged in retirement planning while they were employed, the almost exclusive area was financial planning; a large segment had made no plans for their retirement. One retired man's biggest adjustment was spending time with his wife; one retired woman found retirement an opportunity for relaxed companionship with her husband. What this suggests is there are no simple patterns of retirement.

There were areas of agreement: Most found their work interesting, meaningful and a major interest in their lives. About half of the group looked forward to retirement, the major concern being financial. More than half indicated their feelings toward the job had changed about three years before retiring; the principal causes were changes in the workplace and increased work pressures. These changes were basic to the decision to retire.

Let us review the results of these retirements. What happened when these men and women left their jobs—what were their adjustments, the pleasures, the pitfalls, their advice to others. Again, will we find common patterns?

The majority stated they did not encounter any particular problems in retirement. Those who experienced some difficulty, of a brief or lasting nature, spoke of spousal conflict—communication, spending time together, confusion over the marital role compared to working. Other discordant sources were financial problems, health matters, feelings of uselessness and accepting mandatory retirement.

The single retirement pleasure mentioned most frequently was freedom—freedom to make decisions and the liberty to select enjoyable options. Closely allied with freedom was the relief from stress, pressure and the absence of regimentation resulting in a more leisurely way of life. Other agreeable aspects included more time for spousal relationships and family, opportunities to seek new challenges, time to travel and to enjoy the simple life.

Those few who spoke of pitfalls or difficulty in their retirement living mentioned financial stress and concerns about inflation, a loss of structure for those strongly work oriented and some spousal conflict.

The main thrust of the retirees' advice to others related to retirement activities. Their suggestions ranged from keeping busy full time, being active, to selecting those activities which give some purpose to life. Financial planning was suggested: avoiding debt, living according to one's income and starting a savings program as early as possible. The idea of looking ahead, engaging in some retirement planning, was proposed.

What may be concluded from this group of retirees? Most of those I interviewed, with rare exception, had made their peace with retirement. They were pleased with their new lifestyle, hardly different from the old except in the pace of their living. They appreciated the opportunity to select options with the abundance of available time. The retirees were ready to enjoy the fruit of their labor. It should not be surprising that their conversations varied so greatly about their perceptions of retirement; this was, after all, an untrodden path. It was a new direction in their lives and would be as unique as their lives in the past.

The question remains: From these interviews, was there a consensus of action, opinion or outcome from which we may draw counsel?

One matter is clear: How we face retirement is another phase of our development as a person. If our pattern, while we worked, was devoted to serving the many roles of spouse, parent, community member, parent to our parents, nothing will change in this respect. Our responsibility will be lightened when we leave the job, but our participation and concern for others continues. If we were curious about our world, eager for new experience, this enthusiasm for living will not be diminished by retirement.

Is planning the answer? There is no question that retirement planning has merit, but it is not the be-all and end-all to a satisfying retirement. Preparation for the future is beneficial in that you have a game plan of sorts for the future. In truth, most people have a fairly accurate estimate of what their retirement income will be, based on a real or assumed degree of financial security. This financial base is the core of their decision-making and relates to every aspect of their retirement living. Other facets of retirement planning—living arrangements, the use of time for leisure interests and community service, attending to legal and estate matters—may be appropriately decided after retirement. What is called for is recognition of changes in one's life down the road, i.e., diminished physical vigor, often fewer friendships, some constriction in activities and the loss of one's spouse. This awareness of change, revealed from broad retirement planning, suggests the value of thinking through your personal circumstances to develop ways and means to accommodate to these changes.

A rewarding retirement for most people is based on a readiness to retire along with a continuity of involvement. This readiness reflects an attitude of optimism that the days ahead appear pleasurable with a pace of the retiree's own design. The link of the past and present suggests that one's lifestyle essentially remains the same; with the exception of work, responsibilities—relationships—and activities go forward. Now, with the voluntary decision to retire, the reality of retirement is a continuity of daily involvement with the familiar and opportunities, if we so desire, for new sights, sounds, and challenges.

Retirement is a life event for which many may give thanks. If we are not wiser as we age, we are more accepting and appreciative of the fact we have survived the struggle of everyday living. We may not have built the biggest building, composed a symphony, or written the great American novel, but we have made our way in the world. Now, with the blessing of health, we face retirement as we have met life: with the conviction of survivors, with the confidence to make the most of the years ahead.

References

AARP. *A profile of older Americans: 1991*. Washington, D.C.: American Association of Retired Persons.

Albee, G. W. (1987). The rationale and need for primary prevention. In S. E. Goldston (Ed.), *Concepts of primary prevention: A framework for program development*. California Department of Mental Health, Office of Prevention.

Atchley, R. C. (1976). *The sociology of retirement*. Cambridge, Mass.: Schenkman.

Back, K. W. (1969). The ambiguity of retirement. In E. W. Busse & E. Pfeiffer (Eds.), *Behavior and adaptation in late life*. Boston: Little, Brown.

Banziger, G. (1979). Toward an age-irrelevant society. In D. Baugher (chair), *Growing old in America: Psychological and policy issues*, Presentation as part of a symposium, sponsored by the Society for the Psychological Study of Social Issues, Annual Convention of the American Psychological Association, New York, September.

Bunzel, J. T. (1972). Note on the history of a concept—Gerontophobia. *Gerontologist, 12* (2) 116.

Butler, R. N. (1969). The effects of medical and health progress on the social and economic aspects of the life cycle. *Industrial Gerontology, 1*, 1–9.

Butler, R. N., & Lewis, M. I. (1973). *Aging and mental health*. St. Louis: C. V. Mosby Co.

Cottle, T. J. (1978). *Private lives and public accounts*, New York: New Viewpoints, A Division of Franklin Watts.

Cowen, E. L., & Zax, M. (1967). Mental health fields today: Issues and problems. In E. L. Cowen, E. A. Gardner, & M. Zax (Eds.), *Emer-

gent approaches to mental health problems, pp. 3-29. New York: Appelton, Century, Crofts.

Danish, S. J., & D'Augelli, A. B. (1980). Promoting competence and enhancing development through life development intervention. In L. A. Bond & J. C. Rosen (Eds.), *Competence and coping during adulthood.* Published for the Vermont Conference on the Primary Prevention of Psychopathology, Hanover, New Hampshire, University Press of New England.

Darrow, R. W. (1975, December 28). Employee communication—neglected need. *The New York Times*, p. 10.

Erikson, E. H. (1975). *Life history and historical moment.* New York: Norton, 1975.

Hirschowitz, R. H. (1974). The human aspects of managing transition. *Personnel, 51* (3), 12.

Institute of Gerontology. (1988). *Aging workforce.* Wayne State University Conference.

Institute for Social Research. (1974). *Measuring the quality of life in America.* The University of Michigan.

Kline, C. (1975). The socialization process of women. *Gerontologist, 15* (6), 484.

Marcus, A. D. (1989, December 12). Courts uphold oral pledges of lifetime employment. *The Wall Street Journal*, pp. B1-7.

Montgomery, R., & Borgatta, E. (1986). Plausible theories and the development of scientific theory. *Research on Aging, 8* (4), 600.

Overholser, R. V., & Randolph, E. (1979). Start young: How to age with health, productivity and happiness [interview with Erdman Palmore]. *Family Circle, 92* (2), 2.

Palmore, E. B., Burchett, B. M., Fillenbaum, G. G., George, L. K., & Wallman, L. M. (1985). *Retirement causes and consequences.* New York: Springer Publishing Co.

Piaget, J. (1952). *The origins of intelligence in children.* New York: International Universities Press.

Prentis, R. S. (1975, December). Who helps the retiree retire? *Pension World*, pp. 52-56.

Prentis, R. S. (1980). White-collar working women's perception of retirement. *The Gerontologist, 20* (1), 90-95.

Rubin, L. B. (1980). The empty nest: beginning or ending? In L. A. Bond & J. C. Rosen (Eds.), *Competence and Coping During Adulthood.* Published for the Vermont Conference on the Primary Prevention of Psychopathology, Hanover, New Hampshire, University Press of New England.

Streib, G. F., & Schneider, C. J. (1971). *Retirement in American society—impact and process.* Ithaca and London: Cornell University Press.

Suin, R. M. (1976, December). How to break the vicious cycle of stress. *Psychology Today*, p. 60.

Tatzmann, M. (1972, September-October). How to prevent retirement shock. *Personnel Administrator*, pp. 45, 47.

The Wall Street Journal (1990, May 31). Marketplace, p. B1.

Index

About the Author

RICHARD S. PRENTIS is an associate at the Institute of Gerontology at Wayne State University. He is a member of the Gerontological Society of America and the Michigan Society of Gerontology, and he has written several articles about retirement.